BEST LADS OF NI.

The illustrations on the front and back cover are copies of originals by Audrey Culling.

Best Lads of Nidderdale

A Compilation by Ken Wilford

William Sessions Limited
York, England

ISBN 1 85072 246 3

Printed in 11 on 12½ point Plantin Typeface
from Author's Disk
by Sessions of York
The Ebor Press
York, England

Levi Gill

November 1870

of 3 or 4 that had been lately built and
therefore they were called the New houses
There is (or was then) a small copse of
wood in front of them but seperated
by a road leading down to the Hall on
one side and the highway on the othe
The next School I went to was one nee
to Bewerley Hall. The building had formerly
been a monastic Chapel. A description of which may
be found in the history of Nidderdale pages 53 & 54 While
at this school, I remember the master telling me I was
the best speller he had in the school. After living at
Bewerly a few years we removed to Pately to a hous
attached to a Public house known by the sign as th
Sholder of mutton: I think it was then the propert
of John Harker of Greenhousile and brother to
Robert Harker of Pately. The house now forms par
of the Public House. After our removal to Pately
I went to the school of John Braife. He afterwards kep
the Post Office at Pately for a great number of years. H
was a man very highly respected. In an accou
book that belonged to my father, which I have

*Copy of fourth page of original document. Style change on line 8 is
discussed on p.19.*

vi

Contents

Chapter   *Page*

Acknowledgements   viii

Introduction   x

1. The Autobiography of Levi Gill, part 1   1

2. Young Men Gone – A Context by Ken Wilford   17

3. The Autobiography of Levi Gill, part 2   33

4. Punishment Fit – A Commentary by Ken Wilford   44

5. Journal of a Voyage by Thomas Blackah   73

6. Extract from *On Greenhow Hill* by Rudyard Kipling   96

7. An Epilogue by Ken Wilford   106

    Index of Persons Mentioned   107

    Index of Places Mentioned   110

Acknowledgements

THE DOCUMENT written by Levi Gill was made available by
Miss Patricia Perry of New York, U.S.A., and her gracious
support has been invaluable. The account by Thomas Blackah of
his journey across the Atlantic was incorporated to add to the base
of first-hand material which has permitted a fresh look at the place
of Nidderdale in society at large in the nineteenth century, as it
appeared to some of the characters who lived there. Mrs. Patricia
Blackah is warmly thanked for her ready agreement that the journal be used in this way. There was also valuable assistance from
Mrs. Anne Ashley Cooper who generously provided information
from items left on the cutting-room floor after completion of her
book *Yorke Country*. The long extract from Rudyard Kipling's *On
Greenhow Hill* is included with the appropriate acknowledgements,
because of his fine description of the life of the lead-miner.

Otherwise the book is based on research of secondary sources,
consulted chiefly at the Reference Libraries of Leeds and
Harrogate, and in the Joanna Dawson Collection housed in the J.E.
Mason Room in the Nidderdale Museum at Pateley Bridge. Use
of the following works is hereby acknowledged:

A History of Nidderdale	edited by Bernard Jennings
History of Nidderdale	Thomas Grainge
Yorke Country	Anne Ashley Cooper
Congregational Churches	Whitehead
The Hill & The Miners	Harald John Lexow Bruff
Dialect Poems and Prose	Thomas Blackah
Bayne of Middlesmoor	Lucas

English Social History	G.M. Trevelyan
Timble Man	Ronald Harker
Washburn Valley Yesterday	David Alred

The pen-and-ink illustrations were drawn by Audrey Culling, and Peter Culling provided technical support on the word-processor.

Other helpers are named in the text, and are warmly thanked.

Introduction

WHEN THE FAMILY of Levi Gill decided to make available for publication his autobiographical notes covering his life from 1824 to 1880, it seemed worthwhile to take the opportunity to set the document in its historical context, and at the same time to bring forward and refresh some of the livelier anecdotes about characters in Nidderdale in the same period. Now that tourism is arguably the most important pro-active industry, second only to that of the provision of commuter- and retirement-homes, it is more and more difficult to visualise the industrial landscape of 150 years ago. The details are passing out of the scope of oral tradition. At a recent spot-check at a meeting of a social club, only one of the 40 members present was actually born in the Dale. The average age of the sample was about 55-60, so their childhood memories are of places elsewhere, even though their affection for Nidderdale may not be in doubt.

Thomas Blackah lived at Hardcastle on Greenhow for much of his life. He was four years younger than Levi, and he described himself as a working miner. He was not a notably successful miner, however, and he supplemented his income by publishing various writings, and by selling knitted items and stationery from the front room of his house. He published for some years a dialect almanack, *T' Nidderdill Olminac*, using the pseudonym "Natty Nydds". His dialect poems and articles are invaluable source-material and his records are supplemented beautifully by the work of Harald John Lexow Bruff who was born in Norway, but lived for much of his later life at Kell House on Greenhow. Bruff was a mining engineer who developed a great affection for Nidderdale, and for Greenhow in particular, and he set down many anecdotes told to him by and about characters who lived in the Dale in the middle years of last century. Both Thomas Blackah and Harald Bruff were devotees of the local dialect, though they never met. Bruff was fascinated by the Scandinavian etymological connections to the extent that it has been necessary to "interpret" some of the source-material to ensure that it is presented with optimum access for a present-day readership.

An attempt has been made to concentrate on anecdotes which seem to be reasonably validated. In the case of Bruff's material in particular, this has meant that some material has been ruled out of court because he often used only first names or nicknames, and rarely gave dates of the incidents described. Levi Gill's autobiography and Thomas Blackah's journal are presented exactly as written by the authors, to retain the full impact of contact with original material. Levi's words are previously unpublished, but Harald Bruff records in his biography of Blackah published in 1937 that "Thomas, deceived by the emigration agent, returned with his tail between his legs and, to justify himself apparently, he wrote and circulated a description of his experiences, still extant, which is a terrible indictment of what was allowed on board the passenger sailing vessels in the year 1857."

As will be seen, the checking of details to ensure reasonable historical accuracy gave rise to some surprising findings, which amount to genuine original insights and interpretations.

K.W. 1999

CHAPTER 1

The Autobiography of Levi Gill
Part 1

The Chief Incidents in the Life of Levi Gill

I WAS BORN MARCH 25th, 1824 in a house attached to the Independent Chapel at Bridge House Gate, a small village situated on the opposite side of the River Nidd to Pateley Bridge. I was the second son, and the fourth child of Edward and Ann Gill. My father was a stone mason by trade and had previous to my birth, and for some years after, acted as foreman for his father, who was a Master mason of Pateley Bridge, and who also was named Edward Gill. I have heard father say that, for his services in that capacity and for Keeping the account books after working hours he had only 2s./- per week.

After my Grandfather ceased business as a Builder my father started on his own account, but there was little enterprise in the place, and the building there was to do was generally of a very plain character, such as a Farm House, Barn or Stables. He also did Gravestones such as Tombstone, Headstone, etc. He was a very neat and expert letter cutter, and made good wages when cutting letters.

The first school I remember going to was at Bridge House Gate; I think it was in some way connected with the church of Pateley. The Master was called "Old Swires". He was then a feeble old man and had been the Schoolmaster there for a great number of years. My father received his education from the same Schoolmaster. "Old Swires" had a son named John Swires who has been Clerk and

1

Sexton at Pateley Church ever since I can remember. I saw him a few years ago and he was then cant [**dialect word meaning cheerful and healthy**] for his age, and attended to his duties. There was a clock in this School that I still remember very well, which I thought was a wonderful piece of mechanism. It would be constructed somewhat similar to the "Old Cuckoo" clocks. Above the dial was a small door beside which stood a man with a sledge hammer over his shoulder. When the clock warned to strike the small door opened and out came a bullock and the man struck the bullock on the head. It falls on its knees but rises again quickly, then the man strikes again, and this is repeated according to the number of hours, when the bullock backs inside and the small door is shut.

We removed from Bridge House Gate to Bewerley into one of Squire Yorke houses. It was one of 3 or 4 that had been lately built and therefore they were called the New houses. There is (or was then) a small copse of wood in front of them but separated by a road leading down to the Hall on one side and the highway on the other. The next School I went to was one near to Bewerley Hall. The building had formerly been a Monastic Chapel, a description of which may be found in the history of Nidderdale Pages 53 & 54. [**William Grainge's "Nidderdale", published in 1863**]. While at this school, I remember the Master telling me I was the best speller he had in the school. After living at Bewerley a few years we removed to Pateley to a house attached to a Public House known by the sign as the *Shoulder of Mutton*. I think it was then the property of John Harker of Greenhow hill and brother to Robert Harker of Pateley. The house now forms part of the Public House. After our removal to Pateley I went to the school of John Scaife. He afterwards kept the Post Office at Pateley for a great number of years. He was a man very highly respected.

In an account book that belonged to my father, which I have, I find the first record of me commencing work, it is in November 1834. It was picking lime out of the Joints of walling, to be pointed with cement, at Thomas Granges Mill, near to where Grandmother Thorp lived at the "Fold". I was very proud of starting to work, but the first day I found there was conditions to it that I had not thought of. It happened thus: betwixt breakfast and dinner I bethought me to go on to Grandmother's to get some bread and butter. She gave me some and I was eating it outside the house and playing about when by and bye I see Father coming towards me. I thought: What is he coming for? It is not dinner time yet. He came up to me and asked what I was after. Oh!, I said. I only came on to Grandmother's for some bread and butter. He then told me that workers did not leave their work to eat, only at meal times, and he had not to repeat that lesson a second time. I find in the account for the work done here my Father received 1s./-. per day for me and 3s./4d for himself.

I will mention here that my Father generally looked well after me of an evening, that I attended to my school lesson. He also taught me the elements of music. I cannot remember beginning to learn the notes of music. I should think I learnt them at the same time as I learnt my alphabet of letters. My Father was a Sunday School teacher at the Independent Chapel at Bridge House Gate and also one of the singers as far back as my memory can go. I had to attend the Sunday School, and the services as well. The Sunday duties were as follows: From 9 to 10.30 school; 10.30 to after 12 service; 1 to 2.30 school; 2.30 service to 4; then home to tea and then chapel service again from 6.30 to 8. No play for us children, during the intervals, if known [**i.e., if observed by the adults**]. Had it not been that I took great pleasure in the singing, the Sundays' duties would have been almost intolerable, for want of a little judicious liberty. William Wilson, my Father, Joseph Clark, Thomas Stones, George Stones and his two daughters (the eldest of these two was in after years my stepmother) were the singers at the chapel. The musical career of Mister William Jackson the Eminent Yorkshire musical composer was commenced at this chapel in connection with the singers of this place. His compositions were: "The Deliverance of Israel from Babylon", an oratorio; "Israel", an oratorio, etc. etc. [**The last two sentences here are lifted from Grainge's Nidderdale, pages 68 and 69**].

I continued to work with my father during the summer months and in the winter I went to the school.

Straw Platting. Previous to me commencing work with my Father, there came a woman to reside in Pateley that understood the business of Straw platting and practised it there, and she taught several of the natives the art. It was introduced into our house by

3

me; my sister and my brother William learnt it. The Straw (Wheat) I believe they got it at the farmers at almost a nominal price. The way it was produced was as follows: One person would take a sheaf of wheat and hold it betwixt their knees, and then one or more would take them by the ears, and draw them out of the sheaf keeping the heads of the corn all together. When their hand was thus full of straw they tied the lot together with straw and when they had got a sufficient quantity, they would be placed on the barn floor with the heads of the corn together and the straw of each bundle in opposite directions, when the corn Thrasher would come and thrash out the corn without bruising the straw. We then cut off the heads of the corn and take the straw home. We then cut off the straw by the first joint and those cut are used for platting, the husk is stripped off and the whitest of them are selected for "whites". The others are to be dyed, black, brown, or green, where the colours are generally used. The straw for whites have to be cleaned and stoved with brimstone. The different platts are made varied from 4 to 8 straws in each platt and the price per 20 yards from 2d. to 3½d. When we got an order from the straw bonnet makers, we got 4d. per 20 yds in a 20 yd. length. There would be some hundreds of ends of straw each of which had to cut off by scissors, and then it had to be pressed or run through a pair of rollers and then neatly folded into a certain shape, and it was then ready for the market. Our chief market was with a shopkeeper at Dallowgill distant some 5 or 6 miles from Pateley, and when you got there you had to take the value of your Platts in his shopgoods. I believe my Father's object in putting us to that business was to train us to industrial habits, for the money value that we made was a mere nothing in comparison to the dirt and confusion it made in the house, and we were glad when the business was given up. The business of Straw Platting at Pateley died away and I think has never been resumed since.

Probably through my father being short of work at home and their family of children now being 6 with a prospect of a further addition, he in the Spring quarter of 1836 went to look for work elsewhere and found it first at Headingly near Leeds, and also sent word that he had got work for me. I went with a carrier named Kit (Christopher) Grange of Bridge House Gate. We started soon after

12 o'clock at night. He did so that he might get back home from Leeds, within the 24 hours, thus saving the price of the Toll Bars one way in a covered Waggon. We arrived early in the day at the building where my Father was working and I started work on the day following. It was customary at that time in our trade for every fresh workman to pay his "footing". For a journeyman it was generally 1s/6d.; if his son was an apprentice 1s/-, and a labourer 1s/-. The other workmen generally contributing 2d. or 3d. each to it and the whole of it spent in Beer. Of course my father had to pay "footings" for both of us and the beer came onto the works in the afternoon at 4 o'clock, the usual time then for stopping for teatime. Up to that time I do not think I had drunk a pint of beer in all my life. My father was late in joining them, and I had drunk two tots (small glasses) when he joined us, and I then had about two more. I sat still until the men rose to resume work. I then got on my legs, but was soon down again. In short I was drunk. My father saw it and took me into the tool house or cabin and there I lay sick for a while, and then fell asleep until 5 o'clock when I went to our lodgings with father. It was a long time after that before I tasted beer again. The system of paying footings in our trade has been abolished some years now.

On the first Saturday I was at Headingly my father took me with him in the evening to see the town of Leeds, and a great treat it was to me, who up to that time had seen no town larger than Pateley Bridge. The splendour of the shops in Briggate, and the width of the streets, the gas light (the first I had seen), the illuminated clock at the top of Briggate and the statue of Queen Anne, then a walk through the butchers' market and through Vicars Croft (then the vegetable and fish market) then there was the splendid colours in the Chemists' shops windows, the wealth in the silversmiths and watchmakers shops. There seemed to me to be an illimitable feast for the eyes, of which I partook freely. If I could have transported myself back to Pateley at once and given a description of what I had seen amongst my playmates, I should have expected to have been looked at as an Hero amongst travellers.

I remember one incident that happened either on that or some other of the Saturday nights after, when my father and me was going down Briggate. My Father was accosted by two Ladies, who inquired how he was. He looked at them but did not speak to them. I enquired if they were two young women who had left Pateley to come and live at Leeds. He said No. Do you know them? No. Why did they speak to you? said I. They are bad women. Bad women? thought I. How does he know they are bad women if he does not know them. They were dressed like ladies as far as I could see, and they had used no bad language. They had only asked him how he was. Why did he call them bad women? I could not solve the problem. I had to leave it for Father Time to solve.

I have since then traversed through the principal streets of London, and of course seen shops that far exceeded for brilliancy and splendour anything that Leeds could produce, but they never yielded to me the pleasure my first visit to Briggate induced. It was a maiden joy never procurable again with the same zest. The first Sunday I was at Headingly, my father took me to some chapel in Leeds. As we were going to the chapel I heard for the first time a chime of Bells rung. They were the Bells of the Parish Church at Leeds. I was very pleased when listening to them. I had to enquire from father when I first heard them, what they were, and how they rung, and how the changes were produced for I had at that time some knowledge of music. In fact I had more then than I have now. He gave me what information he could and I could conceive how it was possible it might be done. I do not remember how long it was we stayed at Headingly, perhaps about two months. I know the buildings were roofed for some time before we left.

I went one day with my father from Headingly to Kirkstall, to see an old friend of his named Stephen Atkinson. He had formerly worked for my Grandfather Gill, and had met with an accident at my Grandfather's quarry, by having one leg caught with a large stone and nearly severed from his body. He had it amputated by the doctor at my Grandfather's house. When the doctors said they should want two men to hold him while they did their work, Stephen said: I shall want no holding. But they insisted and he then said: Well, I will have you, Ned (meaning my father) and no one else. So it was arranged, and my father lay over his chest while they amputated his leg. My father told me that he never moved a limb, save once said "Oh", during the time. When they told him they had finished and my father had removed himself from over his body, he said: Now I'll have a look at the stump. He then sat upright. The sudden effort caused the blood to rush violently and it burst open the blood vessels that had been taken up, and the doctors had to begin their work again, of course causing him more suffering. My father said he was the hardest man he ever saw; he never winched [**dialect meaning winced or flinched**] during the whole of the operation. He seemed much attached to my father and was evidently much affected when we bid him goodbye. I think we never either of us ever saw him after that interview.

We left Headingly to go to work at Bowling, Bradford, to assist at some addition being made at the premises of John Harker, eldest son of Robert Harker of Pateley, the chief of which was to be used for tallow-chandling. The shop was situated nearly opposite the public house by the name of *The Barley Mow Inn*. There was a Mason worked along with us there named Jackey Dacre and I was his labourer. He often reminded me of it in after years by saying: Tha' were once my labourer lad, wasn't tha? I think we completed our work here in about a month. Bradford at that time [**1836**] was a very inferior town to what it is now [**1879**]. I cannot even remember one building in the town that was conspicuous for its architecture or good masonry. Perhaps amongst the then modern buildings, the most striking would be Salem Chapel. As for churches, there was then only two in the whole of what is now called the borough of Bradford, and those were the Old Parish Church and Christ Church. The latter was at the top of Darley St. and has now been pulled down for street improvements. What few warehouses there were at that time were of very plain character, being built of common outside wallstones with plain heads and sills for the windows and doors, and sometimes a light cornice on the top of the building. I think it would be in this year that the shops were built at the end of Market St. (then called New St.). Blackburn Stationers and Moses & Sons Outfitters were occupiers. They were then talked of as first-class buildings. In comparison to other buildings now they are significant for their plainness. One of the great attractions of the town at this time was the Bowling Green; its situation was about where the present Green Mechanics Institute is. There was the *Bowling Inn* with a large open space in front of it and a great deal of standing room at the back, also the *Sun Inn* at the bottom of Ivegate, then called the head Inn of the town.

These two Inns were the principal places where the Coaches started from and returned to, in Bradford. During the whole of the day there was only slight intervals of time betwixt one or more coach going out or others coming in, so that there was generally more or less of a crowd of people sauntering about the Bowling Green. There was no railway into the town then, nor for some years after. There was generally some competitions in the Coach traffic and often a good deal of excitement caused by the coach drivers urging on the horses with the whip to their utmost speed. The commercial coaches were generally conducted with more dignity than those for general passengers, their patrons being generally men in business as Shopkeepers, Manufacturers, Woolstaplers and such like. The coach driver of one of these commercial coaches was – well, he was somebody at that day. But I must leave Bradford for a time and accompany my father to our next place for work which was at Shipley 3 miles distant from Bradford.

The buildings we worked at were cottage houses and the contractor was a native of Pateley named John Harrison and I remember the proprietor of the houses, a tailor Didd. I believe he was a tailor by trade. I remember father and I went one Sunday from Shipley to Manningham to see an intimate friend of my father's named Thomas Stones. He then lived with his wife and family in one of a block of some 8 or 10 houses situated in what was then called Back Manningham. The houses he lived in had a garden in front and faced into the fields. The house he lived in is still there, but the fields that were, are now all streets and houses. We went to chapel twice with Mr. Stones that day and returned to Shipley at night. The Thomas Stones mentioned here came from Pateley and was one of the singers at Bridge House Gate Chapel. I believe my father was his most confident friend. I remember my mother came over to see us while we were working at Shipley, and I think it likely that she brought some news of a prospect of some work to be had at Pateley for we did not stay long at Shipley after her visit, but returned to Pateley later in June and thus terminated my first travels from my native home.

I was much attached to my native home and when I returned to it everybody I did see seemed to me like an old familiar friend. And the wonders I had to relate to my mates! It was glorious to think about, and to see them, as I did in my imagination, listening with intense eagerness, with bright eyes and half-opened mouths. Wasn't I a happy boy for the time being? I do not remember whether the reality of my recital to my mates came up to what my imagination had pictured or not. As it was based on my own feelings only, – probably not. The work that my father had contracted to do at Pateley was to pull down some old houses, the new ones to be shops at front, with dwelling houses at the back, 2 in number. The proprietor of the buildings was John Harker, Greenhouse Hill, a village distant from Pateley about 3 miles. I will here give an extract from the history of Nidderdale [**Grainge, page 195**].

> "The village of Greenhouse Hill is situated on the sides of the turnpike road leading from Shipton to Pately Bridge at a distance about 3 miles from the latter place and at an elevation of above 1000 feet above it, the situation is harsh and bleak exposed to the wind in all quarters and possessing from its elevation a naturally cold climate. The church is believed to stand on the highest ground of any church in England, being upwards of 1300 feet above the level of the sea."

The church was built in 1857, James Paley of New York [**in Nidderdale**] was contractor for the Mason work. The church was consecrated in 1858. My father commenced his contract with energy and soon engaged some men to assist in pulling down the old buildings, and then in lining the cellars. My father had noticed the sort of stone that was used in making inside partitions was from Bradford and Shipley, and found out that the stone they were cut from at the quarries, was at the Pateley quarries thrown away as refuse. As he required a great many inside parpoints [**parpents being small stone pieces for use in partition walls**] he got leave to take what he wished from the refuse heap. He got what he required and I think he and I dressed all we required. The parpoints that had been used at Pateley previous to this had been made from sandstone, dressed with a pick. They were generally 5 or 6 inches in width and from 2 inch to 6 in length. They were awkward stones to wall, being unwieldy. The new parpoints were handy to

9

wall and made a stronger wall than the other; they would vary in thickness from 1½ to 4 or 5 inch. They were made from shreds of flags or from stones that would not make a flag.

My brother William commenced work at these houses, and my Grandfather Gill worked at them. He was walling insides when at work. I think it likely that this would be the last place that he worked at his trade. He would then be 74 years of age. When the weather was fine my brother William and I worked as mason's labourers, at such jobs as riddling lime and mixing it into mortar, and then carrying it on a board on our heads. We also had to carry to the masons, wallstone fillings, etc. When the weather was wet, I worked at the banker [**a stone bench used for dressing stones**] with mallet and chisel. The new buildings progressed favourably up to Tuesday the 9th of August 1836. We had then got the chamber floors on, and had put up the first scaffold above the chamber floor at the back part of the houses. We then began to load the scaffold, principally the inside one, by the ladder in what was called hand-over-head style. It is done in the following manner:- There is a ladder placed to reach up the scaffold. One man then stands with his feet on perhaps the first stave of the ladder; the next one above him with his feet on the stave above, level with the head of the one below, and so on until there are as many as required to reach the scaffold, the topmost man on the ladder placing the stone on the scaffold. There is then one on the scaffold to distribute them about. The stones about to be handed up are brought to the foot of the ladder, and a man on the ground hands them to the first man on the ladder. On this occasion I think my Father was on the ground, and I was the distributor on the scaffold. All went on well until we had nearly completed the lot that was to come up, when we heard the Church clock strike 12 (our dinner-time). As there were only 2 or 3 stones left, one man said to send them while we are here. The last stone was coming up when: Crash! Crash! and down came the whole of the Scaffolding and the stones sent up, the ladder thrown down and the men that was on it. I fell down with the inside scaffold and among the great bulk of stones. Catching at one of the joists in my fall, but not able to retain my hold, I fell into the cellar steps amongst a shower of stones. When all was quiet I found myself in a kneeling position on the steps. Perfectly benumbed as regards my feelings, I had not the slightest pain about me.

The first man who came to my assistance was my father who immediately took me up in his arms and carried me home. There was a great crowd of people about and I heard one say: "Poor lad. He's one leg broke." Which caused me to look at them, and I could see one foot dangling about and I had no control over it. I looked into my father's face as he carried me in his arms and I noticed how white he was, no doubt from excitement and fear for me. When my father entered the house, I noticed that the table was laid for dinner and a large pie in the centre of it. I remember I was very hungry just before the accident, and when I saw the dinner laid ready I regretted I had not to partake of it. My mother got to know of the accident before my arrival home, and was going about the house frantic with grief, exclaiming: "Oh, my lad, my lad, the best lad I had. What shall I do?" My father took me up into the bedroom, and Doctor Warburton was with me in a few minutes. I was undressed and put to bed and my leg examined, when it was found to be a compound fracture of the right leg betwixt the knee and the ankle. The calf of the leg was badly crushed; the doctor had to use the needle to sew up the flesh. I felt the needle as it penetrated through, and that was the first feeling since my fall. Inflammation and swelling set in at once, and in a few hours I was feverish and insensible. They tried by poulticing to reduce the swelling and inflammation, but it was ineffectual, and the following day, Wednesday, Doctor Warburton brought with him Old Doctor Strodder, and their opinion was there was no chance of saving the leg and advised amputation at once. My father would not consent to that as long as there was any hope at all. On the Thursday, mortification [**gangrene**] set in, and that cut off all hope of the leg being saved, when my father gave his consent to amputation. The doctor then told him that it would depend on whether the mortification ceased before it reached my body, whether my life would be saved or not. On the Saturday the mortification ceased a little below the knee-joint, when arrangements were made for it to be cut off on the Sunday.

With the exception of some slight intervals I was insensible the whole of the time since the accident, which was fortunate in one

11

sense as I was saved the mental anguish I should have had in thinking of the suffering I had to undergo. The use of chloroform was then unknown. The operation of amputation was performed by Doctor Warburton and his son Joseph [**in fact, Levi names the Warburtons the wrong way round; Joseph was the father of Edward**] and a young doctor named Sugden then practising as assistant to Doctor Warburton. (The Doctor Sugden mentioned here some years after this settled at Manningham and established a successful business; he died there some three or four years ago. [**i.e. about 1875**]). The old Doctor Strodder was also there. His duty was, I think, to engage my attention by talking to me, and administering stimulants when required. There were also two men selected to hold me still if required. They were my Uncle Thorp and James Busfield, a Saddler. The last named turned sick at the early part of the operation and had to leave the room. There was no female attendant; my mother went to her mother's house to be out of the way while the operation,was executed, and my father went out of town on to the moor. I believe it was a terrible trial for them on that day.

The doctors commenced their work about 2 o'clock on Sunday, August 14th. 1836, and I heard them say afterwards that they completed it in 17 minutes. I was in a state of insensibility when they took me out of bed and placed me on a table to be operated on. The first pain I felt was caused by something they put round my thigh near to the body, and they screwed it up so tight that it stopped the blood from circulating any lower than where it was fixed. The pain caused by this was intense, and I think was little exceeded by anything that took place afterwards. I had now recovered consciously my mind and feelings, and gave vent to my disapproval of the proceedings going on by saying "Oh!" as loud as I could. But I did not struggle or kick about any, which was better for both them and me.

The old Doctor in the meantime was trying to attract [**distract**] my attention by asking me such questions as : "How old are you? Whose school did you go to last? How did you like the schoolmaster?" etc., etc., all of which questions I simply answered. The Doctor made a slight mistake when sawing the bone. When about to cover the stump, he discovered that the bone was too long and he had to saw another piece off. With that exception I believe the operation was well executed. After the completion of the operation I was lifted into bed and was soon insensible to all around me. I continued in that state for several days more or less. My mother was a tender and kind nurse to me, both night and day, such as only a mother can be.

After the feverish symptoms were reduced I progressed favourably and was then allowed to have visitors. Plenty of my play-mates were anxious to see me, and most of them did so at inter-vals. I think William Snow and Joseph Ingleby were my most frequent visitors. Wm. Snow lent me a watch to amuse me during the time I was confined to my bed. The neighbours were generally kind to me and seldom came empty-handed. I soon accumulated a surplus stock of all kinds of spices [**sweets**] and the sixpences and shillings I had given to me amounted to nearly a pound, the whole of which my mother said was my own, and I was to spend in anything I liked. I decided to buy my mother two dresses with the money, and did so. The giver and receiver were alike pleased. Mrs. Dunn, then the landlady of the *Crown Inn*, presented me with a bottle of wine. She said: "I miss your voice among the singers at the Chapel, Levi, but I hope to hear it again." Mrs. Dickenson, wife of Jacky Dickenson, landlord of the *Shoulder of Mutton Inn* was one of my frequent visitors. I was always glad to see her as she was a cheerful and pleasant talker. Two of my cousins from Westend came to see me, Cousins Edwin and Nelson Gill, during the time I was in bed. In a small place like Pateley Bridge there is more active sympathy felt in cases of this sort than in large towns. In the former each person knows all the others, whereas in the other, people scarcely know their next door neighbour. I went on a visit to Pateley last August 1878 and more than one of the natives said to me: "Ah! Levi, I remember the day you met with that accident, as well as if it was yesterday."

During the time I lay in bed, the building I had been working at was progressing, and by the time they had got the timbers on for the roof, I had improved so much that I was taken out of bed and placed in a chair by the window of the room I lay in, where I could see the roof of the new building, which my father and his workmen were going to celebrate by what is called 'rearing'. At that time and place it was done in the following manner. The proprietor of the building paid for a supper or dinner to each of the workmen working on the 'job' but before the supper or dinner commenced a bottle of wine (oftener water) was suspended from a pole on the ridge of the roof, and near to it a ribbon attached to the pole, perhaps three or four yards long. The workmen all then assembled at a certain place each armed with some stones, with which they intend to smash the suspended bottle. The preference of the first throw is given to the proprietor if he is there. The master mason has the next chance, and then the master joiner, after which the men take their turns, until the bottle is broke. Him who breaks the bottle is entitled to the ribbon. I witnessed this exhibition from the window, and the winner of the ribbon sent it to me as a present. After I recovered so far as to be able to sit up a little my father provided me with a pair of crutches, in the use of which in the course of a few months I became expert. The idea of my being a mason was abandoned by my father and mother, and they came to the conclusion to give me the best education they could afford, so as to qualify myself to be a Schoolmaster or Clerk or some other such employment. The best school about there was conducted by the Rev. Ralph Holgate, an Independent minister, and I believe he arranged with my father to take me on lower terms than his other pupils. He was reputed to be a good scholar, and he was a successful teacher. He was like most of the Schoolmasters at that time in applying the rod as a deterrent for any breach of discipline. I was then a thoughtless and frolicsome youth and often came under his discipline and got well beat with a horse-whip. I made pretty fair progress in learning at school, and went to school until we left Pateley. When I left school I was supposed to understand the theory of Bookkeeping, but I have no doubt I should have a deal more to learn before I could put it into practice. Moreover I never liked the idea of being confined in a room and poring over a lot of figures all day, but as yet I could see no chance of resisting what seemed to be my destiny. My inclination was then to be a mason but I knew I was disqualified for being a mason at Pateley, the work there being mostly heavy and of a plain character.

In the summer of 1838 my father went and got work at Bradford, taking with him my brother William. They both worked for a firm of masons named Moulson; the job was a warehouse in Hall Ings. In August of this year the whole of the family removed from Pateley to Manningham into one of a block of four houses that were owned by Joseph Wood situated in Lumb Lane. They was at that time the first block of houses that were built in that neighbourhood, and are now, and has been for a number of years, a Public House known by the sign of the *Perseverance Hotel*. Very soon after our settlement at Manningham, the four houses built in Belleview, Manningham Lane, was commenced and my father and brother Wm. started to work there. Wm. was working ashlar wallstones by piecework at the price of 4s/9d. per yard and as our house was near to the work I used occasionally to go down and try my hand at chiselling the face of a wallstone, but my father when he saw me would order me off, and tell me to go home and mind my books. But my ambition was to be a mason, and I could see there was a better chance of me being one in a town like Bradford than there was at Pateley. Very reluctantly at last my father consented for me to try what I could do at masoning. I succeeded pretty well and in the course of a month's time I was able to add 8s. or 10s. per week to the exchequer.

I continued at the mason trade all through my working life. The contractor for the first four houses built at Bellevue were Thos. Walton and Isaac Snowden. The latter had two sons working there named Joseph and Thomas Snowden. They had also an apprentice working for them named Sam Rawnsley, a Manningham man, then in his last year of apprenticeship. This job was finished in the spring of 1839. I next went to work at some cottages in Providence St. for Wm. Sugden, a Manningham Contractor, known generally by the name of Bill of Dicks. My wages was 1s/6d. per day. I was working by the day, and the working hours was from 6 in the morning to 6 at night, 2 hours for meal times. There was one young man working there named Septimus Adair, a native of York, but I never heard of him after I left that job. My next place of work was at a new church just commenced at Bowling. [**Bowling is a suburb about one mile from the centre of Bradford, close to Bolling Hall, and not to be confused with the Bowling Green with the coaching connections in the centre of Bradford.**] The Contractors were Stead. John Waugh and his brother James worked there. We were working piece work on pitch face wallstones, and I remember I earned 17s. the first week I worked there. I lodged in Bowling from Saturday until Monday, and then went home. I think it would be at the latter end of the summer that I went to work at Mechanics Institute at the bottom of Leeds Road and opposite the *Junction Inn*. I think the contractors were Leach & Brayshaw. The foreman's name was Jonathan Waddington. James Sutcliffe worked there. He was an apprentice to one Fearnly and was there in his last years. He was left-handed and a good Banker hand. Joseph Hewitt also worked at this job. I knew him afterwards in London. He was subsequently Foreman Mason at Undercliffe Cemetery for a number of years. This Institute was completed and opened I think in 1840.

End of Part one, finished January 8th, 1885

CHAPTER 2
Young Men Gone – A Context

THE IMPORTANCE of the first-hand, subjective nature of biography, journal and diary was neatly stated by Thomas Carlyle when he said that "History is the essence of innumerable biographies". Importance for our understanding of and sympathy with our ancestors, as well as our neighbours, is implied. Carlyle brushed on a broad canvas, and may have had in mind works on the scale of his *Life of Schiller*, written in 1824, the year that Levi Gill was born. Carlyle's own autobiographical allegory *Sartor Resartus* published ten years later was also deeply philosophical, confronting the materialism and mass culture of the time. In complete contrast was the autobiography of Levi Gill, admittedly with its much shorter horizons but with an optimistic philosophy in sympathy with the aspirations and concerns of less privileged people about the time of the Industrial Revolution. Nonetheless, the historical value of such an account is obvious. For example, Levi was happy to be paid in kind at Dallowgill, never dreaming that he was a victim of what history would describe as the exploitation of child labour.

Carlyle was educated at Edinburgh University, became a member of the academic elite, and moved in the highest literary circles, with Coleridge, Hazlitt and others. He lived in fashionable Cheyne Row, London, from 1834 until his death in 1881. Levi Gill was educated in the village schools of Nidderdale, pursued his skilled artisan trade in various towns in England until his death in 1880, and his relatively brief autobiography languished in a box of family papers for more than a century. It seems at first sight to be a curious coincidence that both Carlyle and Gill were sons of

17

stone-masons, but in their century many families would be close to a connection with that trade. Certainly both were influenced by Calvin's doctrines, but otherwise it is probably fair to say that their life-styles could hardly have appeared to be more different, even though they were almost exact contemporaries. Levi composed no outstandingly quotable lines, but his account finds a resonance in Carlyle's words: "Wondrous are the bonds that unite us one and all; whether by the soft binding of Love, or the iron chaining of Necessity ... if now an existing generation of men stand so woven together, not less indissolubly does generation with generation". Thomas Blackah was four years younger than Levi Gill, and until he was about ten he lived within a couple of miles of Levi but there is no evidence that their paths ever crossed. Thomas became a notable writer and poet in Nidderdale, but is not mentioned in Levi's account. Both Thomas and Levi would have understood the validity of the "Where were you when – ?" question.

In December 1998, Miss Patricia Perry of Yonkers, New York, U.S.A., visited the Nidderdale Museum and produced for examination a copy of the document which has been kept in New York for many years in a box along with other family records. The title of the document, "The Chief Incidents in the Life of Levi Gill", is immediately arresting, as is the quality of the handwriting. Even a brief perusal reveals a narrative that unfolds with warmth and authority to record the autobiography of a character who was born in Nidderdale in 1824, made his living as a stone-mason, produced a large family, and obviously wished to leave a record for posterity. The village schools where he was educated could wish for no better tribute to the quality of their instruction than the apparent facility with language displayed by Levi. He may well have made notes over a period before attempting to produce the finished document, but it is of interest that he made good use of William Grainge's *Nidderdale* which was published in 1863 when Levi was in his fortieth year. There are many substantial quotations from Grainge, some being unacknowledged but nonetheless word-for-word. There is with the papers a signature of Levi Gill and the date, November 1871, on a separate sheet which could have signified Levi's completion of Part 1. However, the note at the end of Part 1 of the autobiography states that the document was actually completed in 1885, so although the narrative purports to be in the first person, at least some of the final drafting was after Levi's death in 1880.

The autobiography is in two parts and there are indications in the text that much of the work in Part 2 was done in 1879 which was about a year before Levi died. Levi visited Nidderdale in 1878/9 and it may be that the visit provided an opportunity to meet with family members in the area and collate all available information about his own generation to amplify and extend the record started in Part 1. Had he lived longer, Levi would surely have attempted further recording, particularly with reference to the history and achievements of his own family. It seems out of character that nowhere does he mention his wife Elizabeth and their children. Indeed, Alfred Ward Gill, Levi's fourth son, may have intended to add to Levi's account, but he died in 1886, aged twenty. William Gill Ingham made a copy of the whole document for Alfred Ward Gill, and finished the copying work on January 19th. 1885. It is quite likely that only one or two copies in longhand were made, and it is therefore possible, but not absolutely certain, that the first three pages of the document brought to Pateley are copies of Levi's own hand. The style of the writing changes on the fourth page, and the spelling of "Pateley" becomes "Pately". For consistency, the former has been used throughout this present publication of Levi's script, but otherwise spelling is retained as in the original manuscript, a tribute to Levi's ability in that area. Added explanatory notes are in square brackets and different type-face, but these are few and far between so that the impact of the original document is retained for new readers. Genealogy must be explored to some extent, but is not any longer a primary interest, though it is often tempting, even irresistible, to be side-tracked by what may or not be genealogical or historical clues.

Over the years it seems that the family records have gradually been dispersed without any overall control, but the Family Bible survives, from which the following entries relate to Levi himself:

Levi Gill and Elizabeth Treadwell were married at Heyford Church near Weedon, Northamptonshire on the 3rd. of February 1851, and had the following issue.

19

	Born	*Died*
Clara	Jan'ry 30th. 1853	Sept'ber 14th.1854
Edward	July 19th. 1854	no entry
William	January 28th. 1856	no entry
Matthew	July 27th. 1858	March 13th. 1886
Jane	April 1st. 1860	no entry
Alice	April 20th. 1862	no entry
Elizabeth	February 16th. 1864	no entry
Alfred Ward	Nov'ber 23rd. 1865	Nov'ber 16th. 1886
Ann	February 10th. 1868	no entry
John Edwin	October 21st. 1869	June 22nd. 1879
Harry	April 2nd. 1871	April 3rd. 1871
Mary Ellen	Oct'er 2nd. 1872	Sept'er 15th. 1873
A boy	February 1st. 1874	Stillborn

Levi's wife, Elizabeth, died on October 21st. 1875, aged 42 years 6 months and 28 days, according to the record, about eighteen months after the stillborn birth of her thirteenth child. Levi himself died on April 28th. 1880, aged 56 years, and five of his children predeceased him, as can be seen from the above list. Two more sons survived Levi by only six years. The sadness occasioned by such a high level of early mortality was no doubt only too familiar experience at all levels of society. Little more than a century earlier, the nation had grieved with wretched Queen Anne who bore seventeen children, only one of whom reached childhood. It was to be many decades more before the medical profession was able to make a consistent impact on this situation. There is no doubt that women did achieve much in society in spite of the heavy burden imposed on the young married women by the frequent pregnancies and the demoralising losses of infants, but surely the full potential of Levi's wife in her society must have been difficult to reach with such a persistent handicap, and the fact that all levels seemed to be equally threatened would make it very difficult for blame to be apportioned. Women needed solace and sympathy, and perhaps found the Wesleyan sermons and hymns more relevant than the sound of slogans shouted by the menfolk who were seeking to alter the established order, particularly just after little Mary Ellen's funeral, and with yet another on the way. Most families lived in "tied" accommodation, i.e. tied to the husbands' work in some way; rent was due weekly, and tenure was subject to one week's notice, which could be applied literally, bairns and all, if one put a financial or social foot wrong. But all these were the accepted parameters at the time, almost diametrically different from 1999, and yet we could still agree with Doctor Johnson about 1760: "How small, of all that human hearts endure, that part that laws or kings can cause or cure."

"Bairn" is not much used in 1999, possibly because of the social baggage acquired down the years. Could those lovely books really have been written by the Brontë bairns?

Levi's eldest son, Edward, married Mary O'Shaughnessey in New York City in 1883, and the following year they produced a son, Edward Levi Joseph, who in 1906 married Ellen Cecilia Slavin. Their daughter married a Mr. Perry and in turn their daughter is the Miss Patricia Perry who brought the information to Nidderdale Museum in 1998, and who is the great-great-great grand-daughter of Levi.

Levi's last years were spent in Halifax, Yorkshire, with his third son, Matthew. The funeral of Levi was at Christ Church, Mount Pellon, Halifax in 1880. Six years later Matthew was also buried at the same church, aged 27. They lived at Hansen Lane and Vickerman Street in the Pellon area of Halifax, but Christ Church was demolished some years ago. As is mentioned above, Levi's account is strangely reticent on details of his meeting with Elizabeth, and on their life together, spent mainly away from Nidderdale but not overseas. He visited his maternal Grandfather in 1845 some months after the death of his Grandmother. He was working in the Kings Cross area of London in 1851, the year of his marriage, but otherwise he leaves no information on his own travels as an adult, though he "continued at the mason trade all through my working life". It is possible that he did not visit Nidderdale from 1851 to 1878, so his motive for setting down his recollections may have been primarily to inform his own family about their roots.

In fact the narrative of Part 1 consists almost entirely of incidents from his life up to the age of about fourteen years only. It is clear that he was an intelligent, capable boy, well able to benefit from his schooling, as well as from the strong formative influence of the family bonded by their skills as stone-masons with the respect this earned them in the community. Another very strong influence was the religious one and Levi tells how the Independent Chapel, with its demanding timetable of Sunday duties, had a major impact on his life and on local affairs in his early years, particularly as it was the focus for an active musical interest at the time at Bridgehousegate. Jennings' *A History of Nidderdale* records that the Independents held similar doctrinal views to the Presbyterians, derived mainly from John Calvin's interpretation of the Scriptures, but had a different form of organisation, each congregation being independent, hence the interchangeable names "Independent" and "Congregational". Presbyterianism as such seems to have faded out completely from Nidderdale by about 1770, but the opening of an Independent Chapel at Grassington in 1811 led to services being held on Greenhow Hill for students in training at Idle (Bradford) Academy for the Independent ministry. Funds were raised by the local lead miners, and the students' work attracted the attention of the lord of Bewerley Manor, John Yorke. He was an Anglican, if not a closet Roman Catholic, but he invited the Independents to preach in the old monastic chapel in Bewerley. John Yorke died in 1813, and the Independents then acquired a site in Bridgehousegate and built Salem Chapel, to seat 600 hearers, according to Grainge, at a cost of £1400. The chapel was opened on July 5th. 1814, but was not formally constituted as a congregational "Church", in the sense of a society of full members, until 1817.

The first minister was Rev. Ralph Holgate, who had been one of the pioneering students preaching at Greenhow and who was later remembered by Levi Gill not least for his use of firm methods to maintain discipline in school. The violence of discipline-keeping has lessened over the years. "Old Swires" was actually William, and shortly before Bridgehousegate school closed in 1979 his great-great-great grand-daughter Muriel Swires rounded off the Swires connection, retiring as a senior teacher. In a delightful lesson on point of view, she remembers one pupil, Carl Foxton, as "rather unruly"; Carl, now, in 1999, a gentle giant of a local stone-mason, recalls thoughtfully that Miss Swires was "fairly strict". Levi's memories of "Sunday duties" would date around 1830, and he claims to have been at school in 1837 studying under Rev. Holgate. Other records state that the school moved from the old chapel in 1831, when William Swires died, and when Levi was seven years old, so Rev. Holgate must have moved over to Pateley by the time he taught Levi the arts of book-keeping. Levi may never have known that Ralph Holgate lost his post as minister in the Congregational church about 1845 for what was judged to be "grossly immoral conduct", though, oddly enough, that conduct was not so reprehensible that Holgate was not able to continue to hold down the post of Clerk to the Pateley Board of Guardians, chaired by John Yorke with George Metcalfe as vice-chair. The Guardians were responsible for the Workhouse, and matters arising.

Charles Dickens could have found material in the Dale for many characters in search of an author, and Holgate might well have been a likely candidate. Dickens was born in 1812 and died in 1870, and he found his Wackford Squeers a few miles north of Richmond, Yorkshire. Had chance taken him to Pateley, he might have created a composite character made up of a fire-and-brimstone preacher who was also a sadist, a pervert, an embezzler, and an arsonist. One of Holgate's successors went bankrupt, another vanished without trace. Records were lost in a fire in 1850, and in the days before double-entry book-keeping was established, it was even easier than in the 20th. century for sums to go missing. An eye-catching alliterative headline in a contemporary tabloid might have been:

Books Burned by Beast of Bewerley & Bridghousegate

Most of this excitement occurred while Levi was out of the Dale, and was in any case the substance mainly of nine-day wonder gossip, so Levi may well never have known of the fall from grace of his erstwhile mentor.

Mention of double-entry book-keeping is a reminder that this system of basic accounting was invented by Edward Thomas Jones who was born in 1767 and was a great-uncle of Rev. Garnett-Jones, a resident of Wilsill for the later years of his life. "Garnett" was a much-loved character who was in the classic mould of the scholar-parson. He married a daughter of Archdeacon Bartlett of Ripon, Peggy, aged 90 in 1999. They knew Harald Bruff well; he lent them his Greenhow home, Keld or Kell House, for their honeymoon in 1932. "Garnett" had a double who also spent his later retirement years in Wilsill about 1980. The double was the renowned accompanist, Ernest Lush, and he and Garnett really did look alike; even Peggy thought so. Ernest died in 1988, aged 80, and was one of a small but steady stream of residents who have achieved celebrity and some degree of fortune elsewhere but have chosen to retire to the peace and tranquillity of Nidderdale, bringing with them their necessary means of support. As the millennium approaches the need for a quite delicate balance is becoming apparent, to ensure a viable economy alongside an acceptable population-profile. Taking in each others' washing is, as ever, not a serious option, but – the traffic!!

By the north doorway of the old Church of St. Mary above Pateley Bridge an altar tomb stands to the memory of Christopher, died 1756, and Bridget Benson who were the great grandparents of the Most Reverend Edward White Benson, D.D., Archbishop of Canterbury about 1870. This obviously ranks as one of the highly creditable connections, but in general the records of behaviour and achievement by the clergy of all denominations present a very mixed bag, well-described in Jennings' *A History of Nidderdale*. A candidate for top scamp could well be Thomas Furniss who died in 1735 aged 90. He had been curate at St. Mary's for 58 years, and managed to sell off, presumably for private gain, the parsonage house, known as "Priest's Chamber".

Levi went to school first in Bridgehousegate, then in Bewerley, and finally in Pateley, his schooling being completed by 1838 when he went to live in Bradford. In 1833, Bridgehousegate was one of the largest schools in Nidderdale with 105 pupils, about a third of whom paid one penny a week in fees. There were three or four schools in Pateley at that time, including one where Joseph Gill and Ann Gill were teachers, presumably not related to Levi's family. There was also a Joseph Gill, possibly the same man, who had difficulty getting onto the Methodist lay-preachers' list because he was found to be unsure that Jesus was the Son of God. The educational pecking-order was in process of being established. Some locally-born boys went to Eton and to other great schools, but these boys were usually named Ingleby or Yorke or social equals of these

24

families. Sending the boys away to school had social implications, but also had the possible side-effects recorded in *Nicholas Nickleby* and *Tom Brown's Schooldays*. The constant factor was the beating; the question not whether, but by whom.

In the villages such as Bewerley the older youngsters went to school in winter, but were allowed off in the summer months to help with hay-making or whatever other work could be obtained, the great incentive being to augment family incomes. George Bradley lives in Wilsill at the age of 95 (in 1999) and remembers that as a boy of about ten he was paid one penny per tail for rats he caught on the local farms. A year later he was allowed to leave school to become a full-time farm-labourer to assist the War effort of 1915. His mother went to Harrogate every week by pony-and-trap to sell fresh eggs and butter from the farm near Norwood. George was no academic, but he is still very knowledgable on country matters. He recalls with glee that his pocket-knife was borrowed by his teacher to sharpen the class pencils. The finely-honed blade drew from the teacher the comment: "That is a sharp knife for a dull boy!" In his lifetime he has snared rabbits and trapped moles by the hundred.

There is no record of what happened to the clock remembered by Levi. It might have been made in Pateley; clock-making was almost a cottage industry about that time, and the seemingly complicated movements of bullock and sledge-hammer would be well within the skills of the local clockmaker, accustomed to the "rocking-dial" clocks. The industry survives in Pateley, but is limited to repairs and dealing in antique specimens. Affordable clocks were to some extent a by-product of the Industrial Revolution, just as standard time became necessary when railway timetables began to exert an influence. The Snow family made clocks in Pateley in the years from 1780, and there is a record of the birth of a Richard Snow in 1824 in Pateley, quite possibly the same young Snow who visited Levi during his convalescence, and lent him a watch to help him to while away the time. On that occasion young Snow was accompanied by a young Ingleby, a member of a well-connected local family, perhaps a reflection of the general concern and sympathy at the time of the accident to the grandson of the respected master-mason.

Like Pateley, Otley also had a clockmaking tradition, and so, even more notably, had Skipton. Each maker could probably turn out two or more clocks per week, although numbers are uncertain. Specialist suppliers of such items as dials sprang up in places like Birmingham; the reference number 892 on the face of the long-case clock made by Blakeborough of Pateley Bridge, now standing in Nidderdale Museum, may be the dial-maker's number, or may be Blakeborough's number in a batch-sequence started arbitrarily by Blakeborough. It does not mean that 900 long-case clocks were made and sold by one of the two Pateley clockmakers. The importance of the time-signalling by the church clock-chimes is aptly illustrated by Levi, working 10 hours per day for six days per week, paid by the hour but with no thought of giving less than full value.

Levi mentions William Jackson, the eminent Yorkshire musician, who was born at Masham in 1815, and later attended a "boarding school at Pateley Bridge". He was already able to play the fife when he got to Pateley, but he learnt the Sol-fa system with the singers at Salem Chapel, and studied the piano with Mr. Wilson of Pateley Bridge. He left school in 1828 and went back to his father's mill and farm at Tanfield, so Levi would know of him probably mainly by repute. William Jackson's career was remarkable, and groups of enthusiasts from Salem Chapel choir would walk from Pateley to Masham to his singing-lessons around 1845-50. By 1852 he was organist at Horton Lane Chapel in boom-town Bradford, then at the zenith of its prosperity. Jackson was a founder-member and also the first conductor of the Bradford Festival Choral Society. He died in 1866, aged 49, but not before he had conducted the Choral Society at Buckingham Palace by command of Queen Victoria. These details are recorded in Whitehead's account of the *Congregational Churches in Yorkshire*, published in 1934. The singers who undertook the 20-mile round trips to William Jackson's lessons at Masham included John Scaife, organist, and William Newbould, conductor, from Salem Chapel at Bridgehousegate. The musical high point for the Salem choir was probably their production of Handel's Messiah in 1885. By 1985, nothing remained, even of the Salem building, though a Newbould memorial stone is set in a wall near the site of the Chapel.

Levi's account of Straw Plaiting is a reminder of the ingenuity of country people of that time in finding sources of income. For landless people the need to contribute to the family exchequer is of very great importance even to this day, and goes some way to explain the strictness of the Game Laws down the years. Levi may well have thought that rabbits, rats, moleskins, plovers' eggs, bilberries, and so on were not worthy of mention, but straw plaiting was unusual, not least because of the market in Dallowgill, and the need to take payment in kind. Peggy Garnett-Jones recalls a visit to Dallow by bicycle about 1942 when the local straw-plaiting industry was mentioned. The oral tradition had it that an enterprising trader in Dallow had found a niche which enabled him to supply some part of the demand from the bonnet-industry in Luton. The same enterprise also included besoms. Both industries, besom and plaits, relied on a source of cheap labour and are long dead, but the account by Levi is substantiated. Changes in the road layout since 1830 have taken Dallowgill well off the beaten track for most residents of Nidderdale. Straw was available locally for Levi in 1834, but it was not many years before cheap imported cereals made cereal-growing in Nidderdale uneconomic.

There are records of more than 1000 acres of oats and wheat being grown in the dale, but short, wet summers made the crops unreliable. Final ripening often had to be by means of drying kilns, sheaves being spread out on the latticed floor, with perforated tiles, of an upper room above a carefully-tended fire. Such kilns were in use even after 1900 and George Bradley who lived at Wydra at that time recalls such drying facilities being available at a mill at Norwood in the Washburn valley, and he describes the use of wooden shovels to turn the crop. Some farmers fed the poorly-ripened cereals to the cattle as winter feed. Older residents of Nidderdale may recall seeing fields of wheat, and crops being threshed, but this was under the economic pressures of the Second World War.

Travelling to Leeds and Bradford with the local carter draws attention to the tolls to be negotiated, and to the existence of concessions rather like the cheap day-return. The financing of the up-grading of lanes passable by men and horses into roads for wheeled vehicles was put in the charge of turnpike trusts in the middle of the eighteenth century. The word "turnpike" means a road with a prepared stone and gravel surface, and the tolls were levied to meet interest charges on capital outlay on initial upgrading work, as well as maintenance costs and administration charges. Toll-bars, often referred to as turnpikes, were manned at strategic locations for collection of the tolls. In effect the Trusts, established by Turnpike Acts of Parliament, permitted the responsibility for financing of roads to be transferred from ratepayers to users. By the time Levi made his first journeys to Leeds and Bradford the tolls were probably reasonably accepted in Nidderdale, but there was serious trouble in some areas when tolls were introduced. In June 1753 rioters set out from Leeds intent on destroying the then new turnpike at Harewood Bridge, and they were confronted by tenants and workmen organised by Edwin Lascelles, first Lord Harewood. The "Leeds Fight" ended temporarily with the dispersal of the rioters, but trouble broke out a week later at the Beeston turnpike, culminating in the reading of the Riot Act by the mayor and the use of soldiers from York. Eight rioters were killed and more died later from wounds.

The road-system was underpinned by the network of Roman roads, supported and extended by the monasteries until the Dissolution, and then after that kept in order by the lords of the manors and castles to facilitate their social and business activities, until the costs of maintenance made necessary the change of approach represented by the Turnpike trusts. The Romans worked Greenhow for lead, as did the monks from Fountains Abbey, and the transport of that and other such heavy cargo required well-built and maintained roads.

Seemingly incredible journeys were on record from pre-Conquest days, e.g. Ripon to Rome and back, on foot for most of the way by most of the parties. There were often evangelical connections but there would also be many secular reasons, with implications for news of opportunities of all kinds. Everybody travelled, worldwide, from time immemorial, and, as writers from Homer to Chaucer and onwards made clear, the roads were usually teeming with characters of all kinds. Footpads and highwaymen were part of the scene, but as usual not so significant as fiction would pretend. However, coaches carrying valuables from London to

Richmond-on-Thames even as late as 1790 would pick up a military escort at Shepherds Bush. In contrast, John Wesley visited Nidderdale seven times without serious hindrance.

Travelling by horse-drawn coach was at its heyday about the time Levi was taken to Leeds by his father. In 1838 there were 130 coaches each day arriving at and departing from Leeds, using the network of turnpike roads with the coaching inns which were the starting-points for the competitive antics of the more extrovert drivers. Anecdotes still survive. A notorious driver in Leeds was one Joe Johnson who terrified some clergymen on the way to a Methodist Conference in Leeds to such an extent that they complained to the coach-owner, Matthew Outhwaite. Johnson was reprimanded but Outhwaite also told him to make sure he beat the competition in the unofficial race back to Wakefield. It is perhaps fair to mention that the work was less congenial on the driver's seat when exposed to a Yorkshire winter, or when a wheel broke.

Many a Hollywood film used sequences based on the exploits of similar characters in the American scenario not many decades later. John Wayne's world-famous celebrity was launched by his appearance in John Ford's *Stagecoach*. Levi lived during the heyday of the coaching inn, and the impression made on the young apprentice-mason by the coachmen at Bradford is not surprising. The *Bowling Green Inn* was adjacent to the present Foster Square in the centre of Bradford, near to Hall Ings where Levi worked on the Mechanics' Institute and other buildings, and close in fact to the railway station (with its waiting-room where Tom Courtenay as Billy in *Billy Liar* waited with Julie Christie for their midnight train to London), which eventually superseded the stage-coach station. Railways were being opened at this time in all parts and they rapidly gained a firm footing, particularly with the introduction of relatively cheap passenger excursions. Harrogate and Knaresborough had rail access to all major centres before 1850, and the line was extended to Pateley Bridge in 1862. In 1870, a day trip to Scarborough was organised for Pateley Feast at a charge of three shillings return for an adult, the first of many such excursions to and from Nidderdale.

In a wider context, the journey made by Stephenson's Rocket in 1825 had signalled the imminent change of status for the stage-coach driver. The Stockton-Darlington line was about seventy miles from Nidderdale. Meanwhile, Sir George Cayley was already working on his inventions about fifty miles away at Brompton Hall, near Scarborough, which resulted in the first recorded powered flight of a heavier-than-air machine in 1853. The power was by tow-ropes; the test-pilot was none other than Sir George's coachman, a very unwilling Jon Appleby.

Levi's account of his first visit to the main thoroughfares of Leeds is memorable. He may never have known how restless the statue of Queen Anne was to be. The white marble creation was first erected in 1713 to decorate the front of the Moot Hall which stood at the top of Briggate. When the road was widened in 1825 the statue was moved to the new court house in Park Row. Three years later, a niche in front of the new Corn Exchange at the top of Briggate was the statue's perch where she was first seen by Levi. New Briggate was constructed later and the statue went to the Town Hall, and then on to the Art Gallery where she can still be viewed on the ground floor in 1999.

The masons' custom of celebrating the completion of a building by "rearing" seems to have no vestigial ceremony. Possibly the mixing of alcohol and stone-throwing caused too many accidents. The completion of a major building project is still acknowledged with a "topping-out" drink, but without great boisterousness. The pecking-order mentioned by Levi, – owner, master-mason, master-joiner, etc. – is not so much in evidence now. Apprenticeships are less formal, but family businesses continue to be significant in the building-trade. The need for trust in one's mates is no doubt a factor. The Foxton family is now in its fourth generation in the stone-masons' trade in Nidderdale. Curiously, William Edgar Foxton suffered an accident not unlike that suffered by Levi Gill, almost exactly one hundred years earlier. Carl Foxton, son of William Edgar, continues the family business, and he confirmed his knowledge of terms used by Levi, e.g. banker and parpoint, the latter having been replaced by use of bricks or pre-fabricated blocks of breeze or concrete. Carl commented on the dangers associated with wooden scaffolding and rope lashings, when the ends of the horizontal pole-supports were inserted in the putlogs, the regular-spaced gaps in the wall under construction.

Rudyard Kipling included in his collection *Life's Handicap*, published in 1891, a short story entitled *On Greenhow Hill* wherein a well-qualified Dr. Warburton, who had attended to Levi after his accident, is featured albeit with name altered to Warbottom. The reference must be to Dr. Edward who was an M.R.C.S., his practice probably mainly supported by fees deriving from the mining and textile companies which would have a regular crop of accidents requiring competent surgery performed on the spot. Diseases and illnesses could probably not be cured in the light of medical knowledge at the time, but at least they could be diagnosed. Dr. Edward served the Dale from the time of leeching, purging, poulticing and vaccination, past cauterisation to early anaesthetics and sterilisation (of instruments), but when he died in 1879 aspirin and immunisation were still twenty years away.

Levi's memories of the Salem Chapel influence find a warming resonance in Kipling's references to the Primitive Methodists, for example: "They talk o' rich folk bein' stuck up and genteel, but for cast-iron pride o' respectability there's naught like poor chapel folk." Kipling's grandfather was the superintendent minister of the Wesleyan circuit from 1847-50, and he lived in Pateley near to St. Cuthbert's. A letter in Rudyard's own hand reveals that his own usage was "Pateley Brigg". *On Greenhow Hill* is essentially a love story, but is a valuable record of the nature of the work undertaken by the miners.

The second part of Levi's account is devoted to recording briefly the histories of his siblings' families. There is a wide range of achievement and failure, and worldwide dispersal, mainly to America and Australia. Robinson Gill was notably successful with his substantial stonemason business in Brooklyn. Levi acknowledges Robinson's interest in making contact with family members, but he was never to know that Robinson paid visits to his old maternal home, Swinsty Hall, and that he financed the building of the Robinson Library and School at Timble in memory of his ancestors, and for the use of the residents of Timble Great and Timble Little, and High and Low Snowden, a cluster of hamlets about eight miles south of Pateley. The maiden name of Robinson's mother was of course Robinson as mentioned by Levi. The School opened in 1892, and Robinson arranged an endowment fund to

31

run the school and the library. The first schoolmistress taught about thirty pupils and also acted as librarian at a salary of £40 per annum. Robinson died in 1897 not quite as wealthy as he had been, and left some financial difficulties; the school finally closed in 1946. Twenty years later, about 1965, the waters of Thruscross reservoir closed over the site of the house where Robinson Gill was born at West End.

Levi would know that his family benefitted from their stone-mason skills, but that even these were not sufficient to support in Nidderdale the population explosion indicated in Levi's lists of cousins. However, they were able to emigrate as skilled artisans, which may help to explain why the traumas of long-distance travel are not mentioned. Large families were the norm, and the pressures to seek fortunes elsewhere were eased by the rapid development of reliable transport from country backwoods to distant boom-towns. A skill such as the Gills had learned assured them of a welcome anywhere, often with pay and rewards beyond their wildest dreams. Yet Levi's account is curiously introverted, as is often the case with autobiographies. He lived through turbulent times but told his story almost without mention of anything but quite close family concerns. Causes of death, unless by violent accident such as strangulation, do not rate a comment, even if the deceased is a young adult.

News travelled slowly to the rural areas; the effects of sudden collapses in prices of commodities would be felt locally, often before the reasons for such collapses were known. Thus although the potato-blight of 1845-46 ruined the Nidderdale crops, the Dale farmers may never have been made aware of the contemporary disaster in Ireland. News of national importance had been disseminated rapidly for many decades, by means of relays, for example, but within twenty years of Levi's birth the railway carried newspapers to all parts, which meant overnight exposure to news of events and opportunities just over the hill and beyond, accessible for a few shillings fare, rather than the many guineas for travel by coach-and-six. At the family-contact level, the impact of the pre-paid penny postage in the 1840's was enormous. There was a Post Office before Sir Rowland Hill's innovation, but the cost had been prohibitive for the travelling workers.

CHAPTER 3

The Autobiography of Levi Gill
Part 2

M Y ANCESTORS as far as I can trace them were all natives of Pateley Bridge, a small market town in the parish and diocese of Ripon, in the West Riding of Yorkshire. It is situated at a distance of 12 miles from Ripon and Masham, 9 from Ripley, 14 from Harrogate (by railway), [**The North Eastern Railway Company commenced work on the branch line from Harrogate to Pateley Bridge in September 1860, and the line opened to traffic on May 1st. 1862**], 17 from Knaresborough, 15 from Shipton and Otley, 32 from York, and 224 from London. On the paternal side of my ancestors, I can trace no further back than my Great Grandfather, named Matthew Gill, a stone mason by trade. He had amongst other sons one named Edward (my Grandfather, also a stone mason) who was married to Elizabeth Nelson and they had the following issue.

	Born	*Married to*
William	Oct'r 6th. 1783	? Robinson
Malley	May 23rd.1786	Anthony Ward
Dorothy	July 4th. 1788	David Bentley
Nanny (Ann)	October 8th.1790	Joseph Bayne
Jane	June 18th. 1793	John Ripley
Elizabeth	Oct'r 14th. 1795	Anthony Ward
Edward	March 10th. 1798	Ann Thorp
Hannah	June 24th. 1800	Unmarried

It will be seen from the above register that my Grandfather had only two sons; both of them learned the trade of stone mason with

33

their father. I may mention here that my Grandfather did a little letter cutting on stone. I think it worth mentioning on account of the method they had at that time of marking the letters on stone, previous to cutting them. He had two Alphabets of letters cut out of iron. They placed the letters required in its proper place and position, and then with a sharp scriber draw a fine line round the iron letter. They used then only Roman and Italic letters. I have got a good many of the iron letters by me that were used by Grandfather and preserved by my father until his death when they came into my possession. My Grandfather had in the days of my boyhood, what was then and there considered an extensive business, he being at that time a Master Mason, Quarryman, and Farmer.

Squire Yorke is by far the largest landowner in Nidderdale. Bewerley Hall, the residence of Squire Yorke, was built by my Grandfather between the years 1815 and 1820. He also built afterwards an extensive block of buildings, comprising Coach houses, Stabling, and Dog Kennels. The Squire kept a Pack of Hounds when I was a boy. My Grandfather also built the Lodge, at the entrance of the park, and the new church at Pateley, the first stone of which was laid Oct. 20th. 1826, and it was opened for service Oct. 7th. 1827. The style is early English. I can remember seeing the church before it was completed. That is the farthest incident my memory can refer to. I should be about 3½ years old when the church was opened. My father, Edward Gill Junr., was acting manager of all the buildings I have mentioned. I think my Grandfather would then reside at a Farm House called Castlestead situated close to the River Nidd and about 1 mile below Pateley Bridge.

At that time Bewerley Hall was being built; it [**i.e. Castlestead, present building erected in 1861-2**] is now the property of George Metcalf Esqr. and he has built himself a nice house, and gardens on the site of the old homestead. While I am thinking about Castlestead, an incident that took place in London has just come to my mind and I will here relate it while I have it on my mind. It was in the year 1851 and I was then working at Kings Cross Railway, the terminus of the Great Northern Railway Co. in London. An elderly mason (working at the same place as I was) came to me one

34

day and said: "I suppose your name is Gill, ain't it?" "Yes." said I, "my name is Gill." "And you are a Yorkshire man, ain't you?" "Yes." said I. "Would you tell me what part of Yorkshire you belong to?" Says I, "I think if I was to tell you, you would not know the place as it is only a small country town." "Perhaps so," said he, "but tell me its name." "Pateley Bridge." said I. He smiled and said "Do you know young Ned Gill?" "Yes. Do you?" said I. "Yes." said he. "Before you did, and old Ned too". He then told me that he served part of an apprenticeship as an improver under my Grandfather and lived with them. His name was Tom Gill. He was no relation to our family. I thought he was an intelligent man of his class of life. Afterwards he often interested me by relating incidents that took place at Pateley while he was there. I well remember one that he told me; I will here relate it. He said, "At the time I was living with your Grandfather, I was considered a pretty good wrestler. Your father was then a tall, strong, and very active young man (unmarried) and both living in one house, he persuaded me to teach him what I could in the art of wrestling. I did so and he was an apt scholar; but when he had got a good share of my skill, and with his superior strength, he used to throw me sometimes, in a way anything but pleasant until I declined to have anything more to do with him in that line. Tom would not stand more than 5 foot 6 ins.; my father was 6 foot 2 in. He was a few years older than my father.

My Grandfather removed from Castlestead to a farm called Bruce house situated on the right side of the road leading to New Bridge from Pateley, about half a mile from the latter place. [**New Bridge crossed the Nidd at Wath about one and a half miles above Pateley, and dated from the sixteenth century.**] He also had a Stone Quarry adjoining close to the Farm. There was plenty of good stone in it, chiefly flags and landings, and he had it at an easy rent but he neglected his business and became a slave to drink. My Grandfather could not, or at any rate did not, master his passion for drink, and he was for some years almost daily drunk, Sundays excepted. My Grandmother Gill's death took place June 2nd. 1831 and in two or three years after that event my Grandfather's career as a tradesman came to a conclusion, by all his effects being sold by auction for the benefit of his creditors. He had then to be dependant for the remainder of his life to his children; his death took place Nov 26th. 1842, aged 80 years. They

35

are both interred in the new Church yard, and a Box Tomb stone erected over them was executed by my Father. The inscription over it recording the death of my Aunt Hannah, I cut. The Tombstone is the first tombstone on the lefthand side as you enter the Churchyard.

My father's brother, William Gill (generally called Will by the family) got married and settled as a farmer and mason at a village called West End. It is about seven miles from Pateley Bridge, and about eight miles from Otley. His wife's maiden name was Robinson. They had a family of six children, four boys and two girls, named respectively Edward, Edwin, Nelson, Robinson, Elizabeth and Mary. All the sons were taught the trade of stone mason. To write all the particulars of these my Cousins, with which I am acquainted, would be too lengthy for my present purposes. But I record a brief sketch of each of them, as my intimacy with that branch of the family has been more frequent than with any of the others.

I will begin with Edward, he being the eldest. He, after leaving home, worked at his trade in several provincial towns, and then went to London where he resided for several years. Part of the time he worked as journeyman. The last three or four years he was there he was a master mason in a small way, doing work mostly for speculative builders. He left London for New York, America, in 1850 and after working there, first as a journeyman and then as Foreman, he commenced business in Brooklyn on his own account. After he had been in business a short time, he took in as a partner his youngest brother Robinson who had gone over to America. They succeeded pretty well for new beginners. But Edward's health failed when he had been in business about two years, and he died there March 24th. 1855, aged 38 years. It might be truly said He was highly respected by all who knew him.

Robinson, after leaving home, took his preliminary canters in a few of the towns in Yorkshire, and then took his flight to America and joined his brother in the business he had initiated, and he has carried it on successfully. Now I believe it is the largest concern of its kind in Brooklyn. He is married and has a family of some four or five boys; he had two daughters but they both died. Nelson also went and joined his brother in America, but his health failed and

36

he returned home only to die. I do not know what age he was when he died. I should judge him from memory to be about 26 years. He was not married. Edwin's life has been a chequered one. After leaving home he worked at various towns in England for some years. Trade fluctuated a good deal at that time and it was difficult to keep in work for any length of time, and I think it would be 1852 that he decided to try America, and he prospered there better than he had done at any previous time.

He left there to come to England en route for Australia in 1854 and I remember him telling me that the last thirty weeks he was there he save 60P. [**The £ sign written by Levi is slightly unusual, but to accumulate clear savings at the rate of £2 per week would be impressive enough to be worthy of mention at that time**]. But the Gold mania was very prevalent at that time and he was infected with it. After staying in England a few weeks he sailed for Australia. Nothing was heard of him for perhaps a dozen years and his (now) only brother Robinson and his two sisters were anxious to know whether he was living or dead. My sister Jane and her husband had emigrated to Australia in 1855, and my father corresponded with them regularly. He also corresponded occasionally with cousin Robinson in America, and he at Robinson's request and expense got my sister to advertise in some of the Australian newspapers for Edwin, and by accident he happened to see one of them. He was about 100 miles away from where my sister lived. He went to my sister and eventually corresponded with his brother.

He had not been successful as a gold digger and was in poor circumstances. Pecuniary arrangements were effected by his brother, and he returned to England. After staying here a few weeks to recruit [**recoup**] himself after his long voyage, he sailed again for America and he commenced working for his brother. Fickler fortune smiled on him at last so far as to give him a chance to replenish his exchequer, and he made good use of the opportunity. The mason trade was good and wages high, and in rather over six years' time he saved as much money as the interest for it when he invested it brings him a decent compensation. He then returned to England, and resides with his eldest sister and her husband as a retired middle-aged gentleman. He is not, nor has ever been, married.

Having now given a brief account of the sons of my Uncle Will, I will now give a briefer account of his two daughters. The eldest, Elizabeth or Betty as she is generally called by the family, was married to a man named Wm. Kendal, by trade a Cartwright and Farmer. They have lived on a farm at Snowden a good number of years. [**Snowden lies about eight miles south of Pateley Bridge on the west side of the valley of the River Washburn.**] They have had only one child, a boy, who lived until he was perhaps 25 years of age, when he died. Cousin Edwin lives with them. The other daughter Mary was married to a man named John Dearden. He was I think originally a wood sawyer, but lately a warehouseman. He was a widower with two boys when he married her, and she has had one child by him, a boy.

I shall briefly record a few things from memory about my father's sisters. Malley the eldest was married to Anthony Ward. He had formerly been a butler and she a housekeeper in a Gentleman's family. When married they took a Public House in Sheffield at West Bar Green where they did a profitable business for more than twenty years. Their family consisted of three sons named William, Edward and Henry, or Bill, Ned and Harry, as they were called at home. Bill was apprenticed to be a Chemist and Druggist in Sheffield. He early started in business for himself and, for anything I know, keeps a shop of that kind yet. I believe he has been a steady man through life, and I fancy would be like his father in keeping a watchful eye on money matters. Ned was a wild shaver and of course was his mother's favourite. After a good many escapades about home, his father had him apprenticed to be a sailor, and I believe his mother was dead when he next came to Sheffield. He led a roving life and eventually died in India, a Soldier. Harry the youngest son was apprenticed to be a general grocer and after he had served his time, his father started him in business (he was then married), but he did not succeed and I never heard how he got on after. He had two children when I heard about him last. Bill was married but his wife did not live long, nor did she leave him any children. I was told that he got a considerable amount of money by his wife.

I cannot refrain from jotting down here what I consider a rather crafty piece of business of my Uncle Ward. I had often heard it said by some members of the family that Ward at one time paid his addresses to my Aunt Elizabeth, previous to him doing so to my Aunt Mally his first wife, but owing to some tiff or other he transferred his affection to the eldest sister, and they were married. Elizabeth still kept in first-class situations and was enabled to save a considerable amount of money, the most of which I believe she intrusted to Ward to invest. I believe he invested wisely and well and of course he knew how much she was worth or thereabouts. She remained unmarried some few years I think, after the death of her sister Mrs. Ward, and then she was married to her sister's husband. I do not know how the law was at that time in regard to marriages of that sort, but they have been and are now illegal. At any rate, they were married, and of course he got the whole of her money. My father used to visit her occasionally, and he told me that she once told him that she had made a mistake in marrying Ward, and hinted pretty plainly that it was her money he wanted more than her.

Aunt Dorothy Bently had a family of five or six boys and two girls. The boys were all "Geelices" [**this term is difficult to trace, but may be a local usage, now obsolete, meaning hired hands, derived from giglet**] of flax the same as their father. Most of them reside in the neighbourhood of New York. Aunt Nanny Bayne had a family of 8 children. There are only four living now (1879). One son, a Joiner by trade, resides at Peterborough and keeps a Public House. The House, I have been told, is his own property. The youngest daughter lives at Pateley and is unmarried. Aunt Jane Ripley had four daughters and one son, and resided at New York, a village about three miles from Pateley. Three of their daughters are married; their only son Nelson remains unmarried. Aunt Hannah remained unmarried all her life and died in April 1868, aged 68 years.

My father, Edward Gill, was married to Ann, daughter of William and Jane Thorp of Pateley Bridge. They had the following children:-

	Born	Married to	Died
Matthew	July 30th. 1818		Aug. 15th. 1820
Mary	June 4th.1820	John Calverley	
Elizabeth	Jan. 22nd. 1822		Dec. 1st. 1823

	Born	Married to	Died
Levi	Mar. 25th. 1824	Elizabeth Treadwell	
William	July 13th. 1826	Graçe Mawson (1)	
		Elizabeth Hick (2)	
John	Feb. 16th. 1829	Emma Bolton	
Ann	Feb. 23rd 1831	John Hawksworth	
Jane	Jan. 11th. 1834	John Tilburn	
Joseph	June 11th. 1836		

Sister Mary's husband was a Woolsorter by trade; they had a family of four children, two sons and two daughters. Edward their eldest son is married but they have no children. He carries on the business of Provision dealer. Their other son John died when he was about 26 years of age. The two daughters are both unmarried.

Brother William learned the trade of stone mason with father. He married for his first wife Grace Mawson; she was a native of Leathley near Otley. Their first child was a girl named Ann Elizabeth, who is now married and has had six children, five of whom are living. Her husband's name is Thomas Ingham, a carpet weaver by trade. They had another child, a boy, but he died in its infancy, and his wife did not survive the child long, and William was left a widower. He got married again, this time to Elizabeth Hick a native of Wakefield and she had some nine or ten children by him. There are now only three of that brood living, Joseph, Herbert, and Jane. Joseph is unmarried and is a Clerk in one of the large breweries at Burton on Trent; Jane is married to a rising young Architect in Halifax named Joseph Leeming. Herbert was a clerk along with his brother, but foolishly enlisted for a soldier. I have no doubt he will get out of it as soon as he can. William died after a short illness June 11th 1867. After a few years his widow was married again, but it proved a mistake for after living together in an uncomfortable way two or three years they separated and I think will never unite again. She is at present (1878) living with her sister at Bristol.

Brother John was apprenticed to be a Mechanic. In 1851 he married Emma Boston. After working at various places for two to three years he finally settled at Saltaire in 1854, where he has worked and resided ever since. They have four sons and one daughter; the two eldest sons, Edward and Harry, are both Mechanics. Sister Ann was married to John Hawksworth, a woolsorter by trade, and has resided in Bradford all her life. Her husband died June 16th. 1876. She has three boys and three girls. The two eldest sons are Cartwrights by trade. The eldest son is named Edward, and the other Thomas, the lastnamed is married. Sister Jane after living in service a few years was married to John Kilburn, he at the time being a shopman for a Corndealer in Bradford. They had one child, a girl, born in Bradford. In 1855 they emigrated to Australia. Their family consists of five girls and two boys.

The eldest girl is married to a young farmer, and they reside in the same locality as my sister and her husband. They lived for several years at Huntley near Sandhurst, Victoria, but within the last few years, they have removed to a plot of land (640 acres), which they have taken from the Government. They have to pay a rental of 10s. per acre for ten years when, if certain improvements be made in the land, it will be their own Freehold Property. They have reaped their first crop (1878) and it was moderately success-ful. Their present address is Pine Grove Farm, Numurkah Post Office, via Shepperton, Victoria, Australia. I suppose it is situated about 100 miles from Sandhurst.

Brother Joseph learnt the trade of stone mason with father. He started roving about early in life, and was soon initiated into drink-ing habits from which he has never been able to extricate himself. He has visited most of the principal towns in England but gener-ally stays longest about Bradford. He has never been married. Sister Sarah was married to John Eyles, a joiner by trade. They had no children, and Sarah died December 19th. 1863, aged 25 years.

I can go no further back than my Grandfather and Grandmother on the maternal side. Grandfather's name was William Thorp (and I believe Grandmother's maiden name was Jane Groves) and he was a handloom weaver by trade. They resided in one of a cluster of three or four houses nestling close to the trees of a small Wood, adjoining to the large one called Guyscliffe Wood. The name of the cluster of houses is called the "Fold". There is a substantially built Farm House close to the "Fold" and a small Mill about two or three hundred yards from the houses, that used to be run for flax spinning. They had water for the motive power of the Mill. It is situated on the opposite side of the River Nidd to where Metcalfe's Flax Mill is, and about half a mile distant from that

41

establishment. Their family consisted of two sons and three daughters. William, I think, was the eldest, and learned the trade of shoemaking. He got married and settled in Pateley Bridge where he had a numerous family of children, but out of the many children they had, there is only one of the brood left at Pateley. There are five of them living at Church, a town in Lancashire. Two of the younger sons, George and Joseph, live in Bradford and are carrying on a large business as Wholesale and Retail Linen Drapers. John, their other son, was by trade a whitesmith, and he was married to a woman named Susey Dougill, and they had two children, a boy and a girl.

Uncle John's death was caused by an accident when at work, by his neckerchief being entangled to a piece of iron that he was turning in a lathe, and he was strangulated before he could be released. I think that would be about the year 1830. Aunt Jane was married to a man named Gill (not our breed of Gills) but I do not know his Christian name. They resided at a Village about 2 miles from Pateley called Wilsill. I think their family consisted of two or three daughters and one son. The other of my aunts, I have forgot her name, was married to a man named Gregory Verity, a Blacksmith by trade, and they resided at Middlesmoor, a Village situated at the top of Nidderdale, and ten miles from Pateley Bridge. The issue of that marriage was two sons named John and William.

I don't know the ages of my Grandfather or Grandmother when they died, but each of them would be more than 70 years. I think Grandmother died in 1845 and Grandfather lived two or three years longer. They were never in affluent circumstances, yet I believe they had a good share of happiness for they were an affectionate couple and I think their affection for each other was intensified as they grew older. I went on a visit to Pateley a few months after the death of my Grandmother. My Grandfather was then living with his son William at Pateley and I have no doubt but they would make him as comfortable as they could. After I had been there some time I invited him to have a walk with me down the side of the River Nidd. We went and I began to ask him the particulars about Grandmother's death. He started to talk with a seemingly determined effort to suppress his emotion, but he did not speak many words before his voice failed and he wept like a child. Poor old man!

42

He had lost his all. What was the world to him without her? If he had a pleasure it was increased by her sharing it with him, or, if in trouble, she was always ready to soothe and console him, and now he felt desolate. There was a void that nothing could fill up, and he longed only to die and be with her. I tried to console him as well as I could, and he eventually came round so that he talked to me about her for a considerable time and I have no doubt derived a melancholy pleasure in relating to me her virtue. I never saw him again after that visit.

Since I wrote the above account, I have received some traditional account of my paternal ancestors from my Cousin Robinson Gill and their accuracy I think cannot be doubted as it came from Robinson's Father to himself, and as he was the eldest of the family he may probably have heard traditions of the family that the younger branches did not. It is as follows. For several generations previous to the birth of my first named ancestor, Matthew Gill, the Gills had resided at Sawley and Grantley, and there had always been a mason, or masons, in each generation. But, Matthew being smaller than the rest of the boys, it was decided by his father that he must be put to some lighter employment than Masoning. The business of a Weaver was chosen for him, and he was apprenticed to it and served his master until he was 21 years of age. He was dissatisfied with the trade of Weaving, and being now free to choose his own way, he decided to sacrifice 7 years of his manhood to be the trade he wished, viz. that of a mason. He accordingly bound himself apprentice a second time, which he faithfully served. He then removed to Pateley Bridge where he carried on the business of Stone Mason, and was the founder of our branch of the "Gills".

His name is down as a Church Warden for Pateley Church in *A History of Nidderdale* in the year 1782. I do not know where Sawley and Grantley are situated, but I think they are at the lower part of Nidderdale. Sawley and Grantley are adjoining villages, situated about midway betwixt Pateley and Ripon. [**The last sentence was presumably added to Levi's text to update the penultimate sentence.**]

The End.

Copied from the History of Levi Gill, for Alfred Ward Gill, his son, by William Gill Ingham. Finished January 19th. 1885.

CHAPTER 4

Punishment Fit

THE SURNAME GILL appears in various Nidderdale records from the 16th. century onwards, and is so widespread that a significant pattern is difficult to discern. Recusant, i.e. undercover Roman Catholic – adherent Gills were identified at Yeadon, near Wath in Nidderdale, in 1604, and some were actually indicted in Knaresborough in 1618. Given the likelihood that individual families were often very large, the reason for a noticeably high proportion of a particular family name in any one sparsely-populated parish must often be explained by the chance incidence of a few families of the appropriate age, i.e. before the children became adults and moved away.

There is more than a hint that Grandfather Edward Gill was in some ways a rather tragic character. He figures not at all in the recognised histories of the time, but his skills were so known that he was master mason in charge of the building of Bewerley Hall and all the subordinate buildings relating to that. The Hall survives only as one of the turret-shaped corner towers, but this and the remaining outbuildings prove the standard of his work. Levi's father, Edward, was unmarried when he was taught wrestling skills by Tom Gill, a lodger, and both these young men lived at the Gill home at the time, in Pateley, about 1812 when Edward was 14. Edward married Ann Thorp in 1817 and their first son, Matthew, died in 1820 by which time Grandfather had already moved on from the desirable site of Castlestead which was referred to by Levi as the "old homestead". There are some intriguing emphases in Levi's text, and a search for explanations produced results in the History of the Bayne family. Lucas implies that Grandfather moved to Bruce House in 1818 or 1819 to make way for his daughter Ann

(Nancy or Nanny, presumably so called to differentiate from daughter-in-law Ann) who had married Joseph Bayne and who had lived at Bewerley when their first child was born. Levi does not mention that Ann was married first to Matthew Stones, and was married to Joseph Bayne in 1817 as a young widow aged 24.

The Bayne family had been associated for many years with Thwaite House on the east side of the Nidd opposite Middlesmoor. The history of this substantial yeoman-farmer family is recorded very fully by Lucas. In return for capital sums at the end of the sixteenth century, the Bayne family and other tenant-farmers in the Dale had been granted very long leases of over 1000 years by the Yorkes assuring them of long-term security of rent and tenure. By 1790, the value of the Thwaite House estate had increased greatly and the Bayne family had a secure economic and social position. It seems that Joseph was in line to, but did not, inherit as the estate was sold by his father, William, about 1815 after some financial difficulties.

Trevelyan comments that between 1790 and 1812, the price of wheat had trebled, causing great difficulties for the poor while bringing prosperity to farmers and land-owners. After 1812 the price of wheat collapsed bringing ruin to many farmers who had altered their systems of cultivation to take advantage of the war-situation when supplies of European corn were not obtainable. The way of life in the rural village was to be critically affected, except where a cushion appeared in the form of employment in the new industries, such as in Nidderdale. The protective Corn Law of 1815 was introduced to restore prosperity to farmers. It was the beginning of interference with market forces in favour of farmers, which has been so divisive over the decades, even to the present time, mainly because of the unpredictable results caused.

The 1812 collapse may have been the main reason for William Bayne's downfall. There are many more ways to lose a fortune than there are ways to skin a cat, but whatever the full story, he left Thwaite House to live with his wife at Pateley sometime before 1817, in which year his wife died. Joseph Bayne, 28 years old in 1815, moved from Thwaite to Bewerley at the same time, but none of these details seems sufficient to have caused such reverberations in the Gill family.

Levi describes the progress of Aunt Nanny Bayne's family in three brief sentences with no mention of Joseph, and this may be because he was not aware of the full story or because there was some embarrassment which Levi was unable to confront. In the normal way a marriage with a substantial member of the Bayne family would have been very acceptable, but the loss of Thwaite House estate changed the terms completely. Lucas carries a very detailed family tree, which has dates for the first child of Joseph and Nancy being born only three days after the marriage. This is contradicted in the text on an adjacent page with the indication that Aunt Nancy's first child was born only six months after her marriage to Joseph. That social embarrassment may have been compounded by a judgement that an appropriate period of mourning for Matthew Stones had not been observed. In addition the financial embarrassment deriving from Thwaite may have had some influence on the rather surprising move to Bruce House by Grandfather. Levi was apparently not fully informed because he guessed that the move to Bruce House was about 1827; in fact it was some years earlier. Whether Grandfather was to any extent driven to drink by these mishaps can now only be a subject for conjecture, but further sadness was later to be caused when Thomas, firstborn of Ann and Joseph Bayne, died unmarried at age 21. Further tensions in the extended family may have been caused by the second marriage of Levi's father to a daughter of George Stones, his colleague in the Salem choir. George would be a relative of Matthew, Nancy's first husband, and presumably a relative of Thomas Stones, also in the Choir, who was visited by Levi and his father in Manningham. The "old homestead" at Castlestead was obtained by the Metcalfes after the death of Joseph Bayne in 1854, and was replaced in 1862/3 by the building which in 1999 still stands on the site.

Attitudes to perceived infringements of social codes are often baffling. Why did Robinson not use his full name for the Library at Timble? It was a great surprise to find, reproduced by Lucas, a letter from Robinson Gill dated 1893 from 106th. Street, New York, to John Baynes, J.P., who had already by that time become a highly-respected Mayor of Ripon, stating, obviously in reply to a direct question:

"Dear Sir, Joseph Bayne was my uncle by marriage, he having married my aunt, Nancy Gill of Pateley Bridge, a sister of my father William Gill. I often visited their house at beautiful Castlestead over fifty years ago. The first time I think was at Nidderdale Feast in 1838, in company with my grandfather Edward Gill. Signed Robinson Gill."

So, more than seventy years after the events, answers were being sought by substantial members of the Bayne family to explain the upheaval at Thwaite about the time of Waterloo. The interest was no doubt re-awakened by news of the visit of the American in 1892 to endow his Library, but one of the unanswered questions may have related to the addition of the 's' to the Bayne surname. In fact, John Baynes was so registered at his birth in 1830 by his father, William Christopher Bayne, the younger brother of Joseph Bayne of Thwaite and, later, of Castlestead. When Thwaite House had to be vacated, brother William Christopher went to live at Ripley, from where in due course John Baynes emerged to make good as a slate merchant in Ripon, and later to serve four terms as Mayor of that city. He would be intrigued to make contact with Robinson Gill with whom he shared an aunt and uncle, but who was obviously, to judge from his letter, not aware of the relationship.

Although both Levi and Robinson were young enough for the family "scandal" to have escaped their knowledge, it is intriguing that they seem almost to say too little. Their dog fails to bark! On the Newbould memorial stone in Bridghousegate there is entered the name John Bayne Newbould, born July 1816. If he was a love-child of Joseph Bayne born less than a year before the latter's marriage to Ann, then the embarrassment would really be understandable, even more so if a Newbould wife rather than an unmarried daughter was the female involved. The parish register entries would permit this interpretation, and it is obvious that there must have been a major upset to cause Grandfather to move out of his "old homestead" to make way for Joseph and Nancy. The Newboulds were stalwarts of the Independent Chapel, very newly-built, and it could be that all concerned agreed that Joseph had to stand by the young widow, but also had to move from the immediate neighbourhood of the cuckolded citizen. Strings may even have been pulled by Squire Yorke, if he was concerned to help cushion the fall from grace of his Thwaite neighbours. Joseph went on to make a living as a farmer at Castlestead, according to Lucas, who adds somewhat enigmatically: "He was described, by some who knew him, as a fine tall man, of commanding appearance, with black hair". A character worthy of, but a little too early for the author, Thomas Hardy, who was born in 1840! Perhaps Levi's father vetoed any mention of Uncle Joseph, or the story was just too much for Levi to cope with when he set down the potted histories of his uncles and aunts. William Gill, father of Robinson, would have had to be a very unusual character not to feel some resentment that he himself was not able in due course to occupy the "house at beautiful Castlestead". And although Robinson was taken by his grandfather to visit his Aunt Nancy, Levi was apparently not similarly treated for he makes no claim ever to have visited Castlestead. It is interesting to note that a Newbould family moved into Bruce House after Grandfather died.

It seems likely that Levi just did not know what happened – it took place in any case about ten years before he was born – because he showed no hesitation about putting the proverbial boot into Uncle Ward who married two sisters for their money. Why was Uncle Ward not called Uncle Tony? Probably because he was regarded as aloof or distinguished for some reason, rather as the head of the family might be called "Father". George Bradley of Wilsill still refers to one of his uncles as Uncle Smith.

It is worth noting that Thwaite was one of the granges, or monastic farmhouses, run by the Cistercian monks of Fountains Abbey, whereas Castlestead is thought to be the best bet for the site of the Roman villa from where the lead-mining operations would be supervised.

Grandfather was 52 years of age in 1815, and as was usual with masons his own family formed the nucleus of his skilled work-force. His son William was 32 in 1815, and Edward, father of Levi, was 17. Some details from the Bewerley Hall Building Accounts have come to light, and these confirm the status of Edward senior, receiving payments for work done by the 25 men he supervised. Apart from his sons, Edward and William, the names were:

John & Stephen Atkinson, Wilfred Buck, David Burgous, John Chambers, George Cowling, John Gillance, Jacob Hardcastle, Joseph Holdsworth, Thomas Holmes, Joseph Horner, George Hunter, John Lofthouse, William Longstaff, Robert Marsden, James Milward, Thomas Nettleton, Dyson & Luke Pedley, Joseph Ransom, John Ripley, George Slinger, and William Trees.

There are pictures of the Hall, standing clear of the trees which now obscure the site. The surviving tower and the stone-work which was transferred to the nearby Abbey Lodge after demolition of the Hall in 1924 attest to the quality of the masons' work. It should be said that the demolition was decided on because of financial constraints within the Yorke family, making upkeep of such a large building insupportable. Fluctuations in the fortunes of the leading families have been mirrored in the state of the fabric of the great houses down the years.

Levi's claim that he himself had cut the lettering for his Aunt Hannah on Grandfather's gravestone was in 1999 not easy to substantiate. Miss Perry had travelled from New York, U.S.A. in 1998 expecting to see the gravestone outside St. Cuthbert's Church as described by Levi, but she went home with the matter unresolved. Fortunately, it was known that there had been some unrecorded transfer of stones in 1970 or thereabouts, which went some way to explaining why the Gill stone was lost to view under a pile of fragments. Appropriately, Reverend Peter Dunbar supervised when Carl Foxton restored the stone to the position claimed for it in Levi's narrative, with lettering exactly as presaged. As for St. Cuthbert's Church, built by Grandfather Edward shortly after he completed the Bewerley Hall contract, Carl Foxton expressed doubt that such a building could have been completed in one year as claimed by Levi. However, the Church records confirm the dates exactly as stated in Levi's account, but make no mention of Edward. It was a great bonus in October 1999 when Peter Dunbar "found" Edward Gill's signature on a stone high up inside the bell-tower of St. Cuthberts.

Did Grandfather Edward Gill at the age of 80 have any other reasons for presenting such a disconsolate figure? There may have been some wounding disappointments as discussed above, but he was surely respected in the Dale for the quality of his workmanship, and no doubt for the quality of his relationships in business and family. He had been financially secure because his income as a stonemason was supplemented by farm earnings and by quarrying earnings. In such areas as Nidderdale, second sources of income were of great importance particularly to tide people over the hard times caused by movements in prices set elsewhere. Thus lead-miners would have access to small acreages of farm-land, and walling and construction work was often provided by local gentry to tide poorer people over the difficult patches. The Three Stoops were built about 1785 by Greenhow lead-miners paid by John Yorke when the price of lead was very low. Philanthropy was not the only motivation for Squire Yorke. Large numbers of able-bodied men without a reasonable source of income could imply a threat to the local social order, and the Yorkes would certainly be wary of any stirrings reminiscent of those which had resulted in the French Revolution. Twenty years after that conflagration the turrets, castellations, and arrow-slits of Bewerley Hall were not intended purely as decoration. The work supervised by Levi's grandfather was started in 1815, the year of Waterloo, and barely three years after the Luddite risings. The Hall may have been the biggest project Grandfather worked on, but his involvement was all too soon not even a footnote. The skills he taught to his sons and grandsons soon had no inspirational outlet in the Dale, and served to accelerate the dispersal of his own family away from their roots.

It is possible that he read, or came to know of, Washington Irving's books about Granada and the Alhambra, which were published about 1832. There is one tale recorded by Irving about a mason, who is of the ilk, that is, poor, hardworking, trustworthy, etc. The story satisfies the mason's dreams. He performs well what seems to be a small but confidential job for a stranger, and the end result is access to a source of treasure beyond his dreams. The tale could have been set anywhere. Irving of course created Rip van Winkle, but he was the son of a career diplomat in the American administration after Independence. He journeyed to Europe and, in effect, discovered the overlain glories of Muslim Spain. He went back to the States in due course, and no doubt travelled in maximum comfort in both directions, dining usually at the Captain's table, an experience rarely enjoyed by stonemasons seeking their fortunes in distant lands.

A master-mason, more than most skilled workers, faced the dilemma of how to obtain remuneration for his work commensurate with the time he spent. He would be contracted to supply materials and an adequate skilled work-force to complete a building such as Bewerley Hall to the architect's specifications. The architect would receive a fee as negotiated with the owner. The master-mason, having no capital to speak of, was paid on a day-work basis on behalf of his work-force. The stress caused by the implied responsibility through busy and slack times, and for industrial accident, injury and illness, must have been daunting. There was little chance of being compensated by occasional coups such as a present-day speculative builder might anticipate. The established system of remuneration for stone-masons reflected the need to keep them involved and committed to producing results of high quality. A fee payable on completion of a building might have encouraged risk-taking, both for personnel and for standard of work. The ideal contracts were for huge projects such as abbeys, castles, and cathedrals, where a mason might find work for two or three generations of his male descendants. Even these projects, on a wider view, carried the seeds of eventual demise for the masons. Armies of masons worked on such projects as the Pyramids, Borobodur, and Angkor Wat. Hagia Sophia, the church of the Holy Wisdom, in Constantinople is the supreme expression of the Byzantine genius for architecture and was completed in six years, an achievement made possible by setting two teams of 5000 masons to build the church from opposite ends. How many more thousands in a myriad occupations were required to support this endeavour? In the seventeenth century, St. Paul's Cathedral took 35 years to complete. In Yucatan, when the economy could no longer support the cost of construction of more pyramids, the problems implied for the stone-mason work-force must have been formidable. In contrast, low-outlay large-return coups were certainly possible for the lead-miners of Greenhow. There is a Gill Shaft, named after an unrelated Gill, situated on Craven Moor about three hundred yards from Stump Cross Caverns. The story was recorded by H.J.L. Bruff in his 1920 publication *T' ill*. (The Hill)

51

Briefly, miners' children were taught early to recognise lead ore and they would collect from the old dumps, and be paid for their finds. Another of the extra sources of family income! Two children found some large lumps of ore in a watering-hole, not on a dump, and reported to their respective fathers who were sufficiently impressed to investigate for themselves. By chance they met at the pond, and they agreed after discussion that there was no chance of the find being of any great significance. One went back to his cottage, but the other, named Gill, cut back down to Bewerley Hall, to the office and was granted a "take note" by the Agent, giving him the right to work the site for lead ore. As he left the office, the other father arrived. He had gone home only to put on his Sunday clothes for his visit to the Agent, but the delay cost him dear. Gill and his sons in eight years cleared £8000 from the site, and were able to buy land in Wharfedale and to become prosperous farmers there. In his account, Bruff does not indicate precisely when these incidents happened but it must have been before 1840, probably even before 1800. Jennings records that in 1867 an old shaft was re-opened near the *Dry Gill Inn*, and it is likely that this was the shaft worked by the Gills who went to Wharfedale on their proceeds before the Inn was built. Bruff was told about the *Dry Gill Public*, also called the *Grouse Inn*, outside which boxing-matches took place, sometimes involving gypsies, known to the Greenhow residents as Grecians, on their perennial tours round the race-tracks, horse-fairs and fairgrounds.

When such finds as those made by the two youngsters were known to be possible, the news of finds in faraway places where the metal was not lead but gold made it easy for young men to decide to emigrate, and it is worth remembering that many of the emigrants had previously reached Nidderdale from places like Wales and Cornwall with their own mining traditions. Mixtures would become fairly turbulent from time to time, particularly under the influence of alcohol, and skills in wrestling and fisticuffs were always useful, as indicated by the account of Levi's meeting at Kings Cross with the unrelated Tom Gill who taught wrestling skills to Levi's father.

These years were the heyday of the bare-knuckle prize-fighter, and local lore has it that Nidderdale had a close encounter with a famous fighter by the name of Bendigo, the "Pride of Nottingham", after whom a town in Australia was named. Bendigo is a derivation from the biblical Abednigo; William Thompson was one of triplets born in 1811, and referred to as Shadrach, Meshach, and Abednigo. In due course William chose to use his nickname as his fighting-name. Pedley Sunter was the keeper of the *Miners' Arms* on Greenhow at the time of this account recorded by Harald Bruff. Pedley was six feet six inches tall in bare feet, with nieves (clenched fists) like hams, a very strong man even by miners' standards. He had a formidable temper and he had been forced to leave the area temporarily to lie low after inflicting significant harm to some wretch who refused to pay for his round. So Sunter stayed for a while near Arthington at the time the Bramhope tunnel was being driven nearby for the Leeds-Harrogate railway. The tunnel is two miles long and was opened in July 1849, and some time before that it seems that Bendigo was staying incognito in the locality in training for a fight in the London area. One major function of the fairground boxing-booth was to provide a supply of cheap, expendable sparring-partners for aspiring contenders, but the booths only became legally possible after the Queensberry Rules were instituted in 1867. Before that, prize-fights were illegal and Bendigo was usually arrested after his fights and paid fines accordingly. Sparring practice was, and still is, vital for pugilists, but when the sport itself was illegal sparring was particularly difficult to arrange. A supply of sparring-partners was known to be available, and could be tapped by picking on likely lads, among strangers in public situations. Whatever the motive, Sunter was in a public-house near Arthington when his pint was knocked over by one of a group of rowdy fellows. Sunter jumped up and flattened the culprit, who was in fact Bendigo, in training and trying to ensnare a useful punch-bag. The pair went outside to finish the fight, but Bendigo had picked the wrong man and ended up senseless on the ground being helped by his minders. Bendigo much later was a born-again Christian and became a preacher. He was known to deal very firmly with hecklers if they goaded him too far, and he may have preached at a Greenhow Chapel at least once. His preaching style was said to be "quaint", but the sight of Bendigo vaulting the pulpit-rail to clear out the nuisance element must have been unforgettable.

The Bendigo connection can be rounded off. The fighter retired in 1850, and in 1851 gold was discovered in substantial quantities in Victoria, Australia, at a location given the name of Bendigo Creek. Later, some local clay deposits led to the development of Bendigo Pottery near the town of Sandhurst, the very place where Levi Gill's sister Jane went in 1855 with her husband, John Kilburn, the woolsorter from Bradford. Levi knew that they were still in the area in 1878, and that his niece was married to a young farmer who had land under a Government scheme, but he could never know that in 1881 Sandhurst was renamed Bendigo. The desire for the name-change probably arose from a reluctance to acquire any possible implied association with the Royal Military College which had moved in 1812 from Great Marlow, Bucks., to Sandhurst near Aldershot. When the Australian decision was made in 1881, a local boxer had just attracted publicity by deciding to fight under the nom de guerre of Bendigo, after the famous old bare-knuckle champion.

The largely-deserted terrain which Greenhow now presents is difficult to reconcile with the scenes described by Harald Bruff, when Greenhow Sports followed Pateley Feast and attracted professional as well as amateur athletes. When the mining was lucrative, labour poured in from places like Wales and Cornwall, to produce volatile mixtures of mutually-incomprehensible young men in peak physical condition, with beer as fuel. The beer was sold at the *Miners' Arms* at Greenhow, as is still the case in 1999. The *Grouse Inn* is referred to above, and, before the railway reached to Pateley Bridge, there was another pub, the *Queen's Head*, at Keld Houses; mine host was Bob Coates, who brought by cart every week a barrel of Harrogate Water to sell at one-and-a-half pence per pint as a cure for hangovers. Inter-group fights took place on the natural terrace outside Eagle Gates, and the road there was, on occasion, "black with struggling men". Such brawling became less likely in later years when comparable influxes of "foreigners" occurred, as, for example, when the dams were built, because temporary housing was built at the sites, and the responsible Leeds and Bradford Corporations could exercise a degree of control both during and after working-hours, though of course there would be the occasional fracas. Bruff records that the physiques among the miners were remarkable. Just before the lead-mining industry began its terminal decline, the population on Greenhow, including Keld and Hardcastle, was about six hundred, and of these some seventy or more stood over six feet in height.

As Bruff records, much of the scuffling took place between locals and newcomers, the latter tending to appear or to disappear in line with the rise and fall in the price of lead. However, many "foreigners" did settle down. One such was a Cornishman, Jamie Pratt, possibly the James who married Betty Kirkbride at Middlesmoor and then brought his new wife to the single-roomed cottage named Carr House, which had at some time been the office of one of the small mining-companies. The local stone was almost as workable as the timber of California, so the log cabin of the latter was equivalent to the stone cottage of the Dale. Jamie made good, and they brought up a family of twenty-three. Large families were the norm; at one time, at Hardcastle, there were fifteen families with an overall average of thirteen children in each. As usual at the time, infant mortality was high and quite arbitrary. George Pratt, a son of Jamie, was married twice. By his first wife he had two children, and by the second, a much younger woman married late in George's life, he had eleven children, of whom not one reached the age of sixteen months.

Unfortunately the most serious grievances of the miners or other workers could not usually be settled by resort to fisticuffs. The mine-owners were not easily approachable direct as the system was based on use of Agents. Sadly, many of these were able to take advantage of miners, villagers, and owners. It was known for covered-up pay-sheets to be signed. Companies went bankrupt after mis-reporting finds of ore; plans of mines were destroyed or stolen so that finds could be exploited later. The less noble aspects of human nature were often revealed. It was said that Pedley Sunter ceased to command local respect after he mis-used information given to him by a traveller that war had been declared between England and Russia, the prelude to the Crimean War. Sunter knew of a miner who worked alone on his take at Dry Gill and who had accumulated a good stock of lead through a period of poor prices. He accepted Sunter's seemingly generous offer paid on the spot in gold sovereigns, but was very disappointed when he heard that

Sunter sold the lead later the same day and made £600 profit. In fact the situation was in many ways not unlike that in the goldfields, the main difference being that lead-mining was worthwhile only if rich lodes were available. There was no panning for alluvial lead. Looking over the near-deserted landscape of Greenhow Hill now in 1999, it is difficult to believe that there are vertical shafts of several hundreds of feet, and tunnels along which pit-ponies were guided, before the economic ore was effectively cleared out. Steam-power developments helped to control underground water, and improved ventilation and lighting extended the life of the industry until the 1880's, but permanent decline set in after that. Ironically, the religious needs on Greenhow were met by the Methodist and Congregational meeting-houses until 1857 when the Anglican church was built, coinciding with the final downturn towards non-viability of the lead mines, and desertion of Greenhow some seventy years later.

The tensions between the denominations were very character-building. A sad tale recorded by Bruff was as follows:

"The two little lads who were blown up were playing about before they went down to the powder magazine in Dry Gill. It was in the old Parson time. The names of the lads were John and Jimmy Bowes, maybe five or six years old, they were sons of the chap who was caretaker down at Jamie when the mines were open. They had about twenty-four kegs of powder from Grassington the day before, and all the kegs would not go into the magazine so five were left outside. One of the kegs had burst, and there was some powder on the ground, and a trail up to the door of the magazine. When the boys tired of play-ing marbles they went on to the moor and must have seen the powder. Anyway, they went and asked the blacksmith to give them a match to burn off some heather, and the fool gave them a match, never thinking about the powder. Next thing there was a terrible explosion and both poor lads were blown into the air. One of them was blown to bits, and the other was not quite dead but died soon after. Their own father was nearby. Pieces were gathered up ever so far away, arms and legs, they were all picked up and put into coffins obtained from Pateley. Then the coffins were taken down to the church, but Parson would not let them be brought into the church, because the bairns had been christened by a lay preacher, their parents being chapel folk. It was no use, the Parson would not have them in the church; we were all of us right mad with the Parson, but he would not budge. In the end he would let the boys stay in the porch, because this was not the church proper, and there they stayed overnight until they could be buried next day. The whole village was raving mad with the Parson. Many never again went to church, except at coronations, and some joined the chapel."

Bruff indicates that this incident was still remembered when he lived at Keld Houses some fifty years later. Sam Dodd is quoted:

"I see from the papers that they let black men and real heathens into Westminster Abbey and St. Paul's Cathedral, yes, and even into the Minster at York, and then to think that two little Christian lads were not good enough to stay in the church overnight, after having been blown to bits. That Parson was not a bad sort as far as he went, but he could not go very far. If that was as far as the Church would let him, what worth the lot of them."

By 1855, nearly all Edward Gill's grandsons were in America or Australia. They could search for opportunities varying in speculative degree, secure in the knowledge that their basic training as stone-masons would cushion them through difficult times. Gold-prospecting was tried, as well as pioneer farming. The granddaughters usually seemed to marry well, i.e. securely, into a wide variety of trades and professions, as detailed in Levi's account. On his mother's side of the family there were fewer stone-masons, but most of the healthy off-spring made good. The attractions of Bradford and the other towns of the West Riding was not easily resisted. As was no doubt to be expected the movement was mainly into manual work, but definitely of the skilled variety. Well before the end of the century, the family was almost completely no longer represented in the Dale.

Levi did not emigrate. His grandson Edward Levi Joseph, son of Levi's eldest son, Edward, was in 1913 the President of the Association of Carvers and Sculptors in New York City. He worked on various mansions on Fifth Avenue, and on the Cathedral of St.

John the Divine. By 1929 he was working in Washington D.C. on the buildings of the Supreme Court and the Library of Congress. Status and wealth were achievable for worthy migrants, but there were some problems of which Levi was probably never aware. These were related to the actual journeys to those lands of opportunity. According to writers such as Baroness Orczy, people like Percy Blakeney, the Scarlet Pimpernel, would "slip across the Channel on the morning tide", but, in reality, the sailing-ships of 1850 often took some time even to slip out of harbour. They could not possibly crash at speed into icebergs, but the food might often be well short of Titanic standards. John Paul Jones wanted to bombard Edinburgh during the American War of Independence, but the wind was persistently awkward and he adjusted his intentions to Berwick, Hartlepools, and finally to Scarborough as he was blown southwards. He lost his ship in an encounter off the Yorkshire coast, but managed to board one of the hostile vessels, and took it over to give a name to the Paul Jones, a formalised dance-ritual involving changes of partners.

A journal by a party from Greenhow gives an idea of the hazards faced by less wealthy travellers. The first-person diary kept by Thomas Blackah is reproduced in the next section of this compilation. He distributed copies after his return in 1858 but the family have welcomed a reminder to a wider public. Two collections of Thomas's other work were published, one in 1868, the other in 1937. In fact, Harald Bruff mentioned the gifted Blackah family, all of whom were very musical. Each played a different instrument so that they could form a complete band. Thomas, says Bruff, was no mean poet, and some of his dialect poems should remain a source of pride to all true Yorkshiremen. Bruff himself was clearly fascinated by the dialect, and in particular by the links with Scandinavian words. His publication of a set of character sketches of Greenhow miners is almost written in dialect, which was treated so seriously by Harald that he gives a list of Errata at the end of the book, including among others:

Page and line detailed, for "seay", read "seeay".
      "   "   for "doosn't", read "darsn't".
Or was it tongue in cheek? We shall never know.

In retrospect, Harald Bruff's praise is fairly extravagant. The Blackahs were very musical, but none of Thomas's poems comes down with a musical setting. Had any done so, we might now be comparing with *The Lincolnshire Poacher*, *The Cornish Floral Dance*, *Ilkla' Moor Baht 'At*, and *Blaydon Races*. It has also to be said that Thomas's enthusiasm for the local dialect has resulted in a fair degree of impenetrability for the average modern reader. However, Thomas's account of his journey to Canada is almost a classic as a record of the fearsome nature of the hurdle to be cleared by those seeking new opportunities overseas. It has to be remembered that only in 1875 did the Merchant Shipping Act begin the necessary improvements, beginning with the Plimsoll Line. Harsh discipline was probably the regime in many cases because crews were aware of the disaster-threatening hazards only a squall away. Hundreds of passengers muttering in foreign tongues and taking short cuts with hygiene only made matters worse. How odd that Thomas did not name his family companions, let alone any other passengers, cabin-class or not.

There was also another, less expensive, passage available to other lands, and that was the free passage accorded to those sentenced to be transported. The Sinclair, or Sinckler, brothers were near-contemporaries who may yet be immortalised by Thomas Blackah in his narrative poem.

Jack Sinclair

Take your time and harken well, and heed my tale,
And ye shall hear what gallant men can live in Nidderdale:
Jack and Lishe Sincler, these were their names,
True mates and brothers, proved at all man games.
Their father was a keeper for a trusty knight,
Old Sir Mathew Wilson, and serves him aright.
Outlaws for hunting these likely lads were made.
Bitterly their father rued, but they were not dismayed.
Far and wide in Nidderdale, Jack and Lishe wrought,
Constables and keepers continually they fought –   10
Never yet in Yorkshire, bred we of the Dane,
Has there lived such lusty lads, nor ever will again.

Trusting fair to treachery at last they were ta'en.
Will you know what make of men all England so defied?
They were men that kept their word, so what did betide;
Lamed none that let them be, drank and wenched little,
Bigged a tumbled wall again so-how the job were kittle;
Fair doers, fain to help farm-folk in lambing-time,
Right men and neighbours, never slack at any time,
Jack was born the elder and bore wit for both –   20
Wit and will, wide awake, keeping clear of scaith,
He was but a little man, but best be aware of him;
Look well into his face and see what ye'll dare with him.
Bound to a clockmaker for his clever hands,
Jack has gone with bow and gun on rich men's lands
Holidays and all days since he he was a nipper;
Sir Charles Appleby sought him for a keeper.
Small birds when they peaked he killed with his arrow,
So young a lad at woodcraft never was his marrow.
All bonnie Nidderdale he ranged in summer time,   30
Menseful and mindful he came to his prime.
Jack could run and leap and all, and wrestle on a green;
Little need there is to tell, for that will soon be seen.
Such a difference appeared in Lishe that was his brother,
Docken favours daisy more than these did one another.
Lishe grew bulkily like an elm tree,
A ruddy lad, round-faced, and dour as he could be.
This had a trade as well, he was a hatter –
Manned it like a mastiff dog framing for a ratter,
A gradely wench at Pateley liked him fair and free,   40
But Jack he lived a bachelor for loyalty.
Take your time and harken well and hold your tongue,
And hear of what these brothers wrought when they were young.
There lived a squire in Nidderdale, his name John Yorke,
Long-faced and little liked for his ill work;
A magistrate and masterly; he owned a main of land,
And swore that Jack and Lishe should rue. He gave command,
Fair means or foul means, down to his Hall
They must e'en be drawn like beasts to a stall.
Lishe is gone a-courting as lightsome as a lark,   50

60

Four black Riponers lay in wait at dark;
These besought their Maker to deal with him alone,
For they said his brother was a devil with a gun.
They were four champions which had each other bound
To do their duty manfully for twenty pound.
Lishe is thinking of his love, and that's no shame,
But they seize and quell him cruelly in the King's name.
Taken all at unawares, he strikes not a blow –
Manacled, to main force Lishe must bow.
"By God! Ye are not Englishmen to deal in such a way: 60
I wish I had my shackles free, and some fair play."
They drew him down upon the stones; he fought with all his might.
But soon they deemed a lion come to rive men in the night.
Jack was at foot play; the wench called him out –
No weapon but his hands he had for that bout,
And thrust in among. Says Lishe, "Guard thy liberty,
For I'm in chains." Jack throttled one: "That shall never be!"
Such a gripper Jack was that all gave way,
And these four champions were naked as the day,
Bothered with their britches. I would give a week   70
If I might see him set about such a merry trick.
He launched one blow to free his young brother,
And cried on him to run; it needs not another.
But Lishe was bitter angry to hear that word,
He thought that he would partly try if help he might afford.
He strained at his manacles, and rose up off the grass,
And downstruck them on a stone – they chinked like glass.
"Well done." said Jack to that: but be not overkeen,
This has been as neat a do as ever yet was seen.
Wielding all wittily, they went their way,   80
For such as fight and run, can fight another day.

This account reveals much more than is apparent at first sight.
Elisha was born in 1810, Jack in 1808, and by 1831 they were
regarded as such serious villains that they were caught, tried, and
sentenced to free passage to Tasmania in a prison-ship. Jack was
then 23, usually carried fire-arms, and had had a price on his head
for some time. The poem suggests that the heavies were not law

officers but were intent on teaching the two lads a lesson, rather than actually trying to arrest them, so the incident may be dated not earlier than 1825, when Elisha would be 15, or possibly a year or two later. In any case, the poet was born in 1828 and certainly never had a close encounter of any kind with the Sinclair brothers before they got back to Nidderdale about 1870.

The venue of the fight described has to meet certain criteria. It has to be outside the built-up area of Pateley, but likely to be frequented late on a summer evening by local youngsters for casual games involving both sexes. Elisha was with his girl-friend who was able to raise the alarm quite promptly to bring Jack from his foot-play, presumably at a kick-about with other lads (line 64). The venue also has to be approachable from the general direction of Ripon with plenty of cover to provide concealment for the snatch-squad. There must also be substantial boulders available for break-ing manacles (line 77). The area around Hole, or Old, Crags on the edge of Pateley Moor at High Wild Carr on the left of the road from Pateley to Dallowgill, along which Levi Gill carried his bun-dles of plaited straw, near the junction with a road to Blazefield and Ripon, is a location which meets the required limits. It was also the piece of land eventually formally allotted under the Enclosure Act of 1845 for the "recreation and exercise for the inhabitants of the township of High and Low Bishopside and neighbourhood".

The Ripon Court records show that they were eventually appre-hended by authorised officers from Kirby Malzeard and Laverton, but the severity of the sentences meted out was not strictly for the poaching but because Jack inflicted a knife-wound on the arm of a gamekeeper in another incident, and then threatened to use a knife on an officer while resisting arrest, and Elisha aided and abetted these felonies. The two brothers were almost certainly in custody for many months before they were sentenced to their journey to the Antipodes in 1831, so Jack had a price on his head for more like eleven months than the eleven years quoted in *Yorke Country*. They could hardly be wanted by the Law at ages 12 and 10, and at the same time claim to be hatters and clockmakers. They found their way back about 39 years later, when Elisha was about sixty years old. Jack survived his brother by some 26 years; he died in 1902, aged 94, a bachelor to the end, in accommodation near the old workhouse between Pateley and Blazefield, a stonesthrow from the venue of his legendary defeat of the Ripon Four. The details of the fight would be an oral tradition which would come to the notice of the poet not before about 1838 when he was aged 10, and it would be a few years before he composed the epic. This time-scale would account for the vagueness of detail about the "trick" by which the hired men were incapacitated (line 71). The main witness, who may have been interviewed in person by Thomas Blackah, would be the comely wench (line 40) who ran for help, and it is understandable that she may well not have realised that Jack used a knife to cut the belts and waistbands of the heavies to put them out of action. No matter how much romantic licence went into the epic, there can be no doubt that Jack was a considerable natural athlete, tough and wiry, and it is sad that nothing seems to be known of his exploits after he served his sentence until he arrived back home in the twilight of his life.

Use of knives by the Sinclairs was the main consideration when they were eventually brought to judgement. The Court records name them as Sinckler a.k.a. Hebden, brothers, as if, possibly, their gamekeeper father had never formalised his relationship, which would give an explanation for the absent father arrangement (line 5). Judith Hebden and Mary Sinkler are listed on one of the Class lists at the Pateley Methodists in 1770 and these ladies may have been grandmothers of Jack. The father worked for Sir Mathew Wilson at Eshton in Airedale. As mentioned above, the two incidents in particular which brought about the downfall of the brothers, occurred when Jack wounded a gamekeeper, using a knife, aided and abetted by Elisha and an accomplice, William Longthorne, not to be confused with Will Longthorn who was born in 1839, seven years after these desperate incidents took place. Law officers later arrested all three, but they were charged also with resisting arrest, Jack's knife again making an appearance.

The two brothers each learned a trade (lines 24, 38) and probably never quite understood why their efforts to supplement their incomes and diets were regarded so casually in 1820 but so seriously in 1830. They had grown up to think that a rabbit caught on Pateley Moor was not different from a rabbit caught in the woods near Bewerley Hall, but they ran foul of the Game Laws introduced shortly after the Duke of Clarence became King William IV in June 1830. Being known poachers they were treated severely to discourage the others, in spite of their young ages.

They lived with their mother in Maltkiln Yard which was near the bottom of Pateley High Street, and very near to a top-hat factory run by Messrs. Henry and John Sinclair in 1822. This establishment, probably one tiny room with a stone sink, a cupboard, and a bench, making hats to orders received from retailers in Leeds et al., was demolished in 1863 to make way for the railway, and may be where Elisha worked at age 12 to gain himself the right eventually to call himself a hatter. Jack may have served his clockmaking apprentice years under Richard Blakeborough who turned out clocks on premises near the Bank at the top of Pateley High Street. There is a photograph in existence of Jack Sinclair as quite an old man posing appropriately with a colleague at the scene of his capture. The massive boulder nearby is identifiable as one of the rocks at the same venue near High Wild Carr. Dayne Swires of Summerbridge currently (1999) has the photograph and carries the oral tradition identifying the rock. What prompted Thomas Blackah to compose his account? Possibly the stimulation of local interest when the recreation ground at High Wild Carr was formally delineated, or even possibly when Jack reappeared in Pateley after serving his sentence and making his way home.

The poem does not speak well of Squire John Yorke (lines 44, 45) but any such yarn needs a hissable villain. In fact, people of Yorke's status would be aware that the Enclosure Acts would be preceded by Game Laws to enable serious poachers and other trespassers to be rounded up to pre-empt violent reaction to the Enclosures. Squire Yorke would also know that the two brothers were able and helpful, friendly and well-liked (lines 15 to 19), and he may well have hoped that a short, sharp shock, and a lecture, backed up by some paid game-keeping duties to supplement their other careers in hats and clocks, would keep them out of big trouble. Jack's prowess with bow and gun came to the attention of a local landowner, no doubt, leading to his being offered a job as gamekeeper, but there seems to be no record of a Sir Charles Appleby (line 27). It is possible that by the time the poet composed his account, recollections were slightly incorrect but that an

Appleby did indeed offer Jack a job on the estate associated with Kell House which stood, and still stands, above Pateley, (not to be confused with the Kell House at Keld Houses near Greenhow). Alternatively, John Bradford, the Squire's agent who lived at Kell House at the time, may have been the contact with the keeper-job offer, but may have been named Appleby in the oral tradition because the Appleby family took over Kell House about 1830 (line 27). The brothers' eventual capture is mentioned in line 13, but is clearly not the main subject of the epic.

There may have been another reason for the poet to speak less than well of Squire Yorke. About 1860, Greenhow School was endowed by John Yorke with £5 per year and "removed from the influence of the Dissenters", causing extended religious dispute, which went on until at least 1878 when letters on the subject to the Nidderdale Herald were penned by Thomas Blackah, who was by this time a leading spokesman for the miners.

Outside London there were no uniformed, salaried police forces until 1856. Law-enforcement was based on a system of enhanced citizens's arrest supervised by Justices of Peace. Suspected offenders were apprehended by capable deputies in return for fees or rewards put up by plaintiffs. After the court proceedings in 1831 it may well be that Jack escaped from custody, because *Yorke Country* records that the local paper ran a headline on March 23rd. 1833:

Capture of a Desperate Character at Ripon.

Trial at York Assizes followed. John Yorke's gamekeeper, Robinson, qualified for the £100 reward, and was given the poacher's gun. Jack Sinclair, then aged 25, was sent to his berth on the prison-ship. John Yorke's son, also John, was then aged six, and "was taught by his father to ride, shoot, and know the moors" as recorded by Mrs. Ann Ashley Cooper, and as a young man he hunted with the York & Ainsty Hunt, and with the Bedale and the Bramham, while Jack and Elisha served their time. There was no riding to hounds on Greenhow because of the risk of falling into mine-workings.

When Jack was taken away to Tasmania the great railway development was still largely on the drawing-board, but by the time he found his way back to his old haunts about 1870, the railway up to Pateley Bridge had already changed the pattern of transport. Oddly, the result for Jack was that the old road to Dallow and Kirby was unchanged, effectively bypassed by the new layout. Pateley Moor was as wild as before he went away, and High Wild Carr much as he remembered except for the addition of a good mileage of dry-stone walls. It was to be many years before the recreation ground was moved to the riverside site. When Jack got off the train after his journey home past the new mills with huge chimneys belching smoke over New York and Glasshouses he found that in Pateley, the living conditions in the High Street were still affected by the open watercourses which received effluent from pigsties and privies. In 1873, Dr. Edward Warburton opined that only the providence of God kept the town free from epidemics, and a year later several deaths from typhoid were recorded. Such conditions were commonplace, however, but were improving in the cities. Thomas Carlyle dined in Chelsea with closed windows if the wind was adverse, but the low point had been passed in London in 1858, the year of the "great stink" when the air near the Thames was virtually unbreathable as the tide rose on a warm, windless day. Oddly enough it was almost exactly 100 years later that London air again became unbreathable in the "great smog". Among the most important early demands placed on the huge Newcomen steam engines was to pump water and sewage along designated underground tunnels to sewage-treatment farms and eventually further out to sea to abate the nuisance which for a while must have threatened major calamity. The River Nidd was subject to considerable fluctuation in level before Gouthwaite reservoir was completed in 1901, and dry summers would emphasise the problem of pollution. The harnessing of the river by the many mills was mainly directed to ensuring a head of water at the site, the main flow being allowed to pass nearby virtually unchecked. The huge volume of stored water at Gouthwaite ensured a power-head for the more demanding textile-mills, and also made possible controlled flushing of effluents.

While Jack was away, the power-structure in the Dale had changed out of all recognition. George Metcalfe was the uncrowned king, in his newly-built palace at Castlestead. He aspired to rank with the financier-industrialists of the period and did very well considering that the hinterland he controlled was essentially limited and unable to provide support for his empire when serious depression took hold. Nidderdale was always bound to be peripheral to the broad industrial bases of the main centres such as Leeds and Bradford. Niche-opportunities must always be the aim in places such as Pateley Bridge, to avoid drastic fluctuations in population and investment. On the face of it, Metcalfe would be a contender for "Best Lad", but any examination of his claim points to the clear winner of that title. A lady, in fact, namely Elizabeth Metcalfe, George's mother, who was about as close as one can get to being a self-made tycoon, a business wizard who controlled interests in farming, flax, and brewing after she was widowed in 1798, until she handed on to her sons in 1850 a sound capital base for them to develop. She was a shrewd operator, and never became overextended. Within ten years of George's death in 1898, his ventures had collapsed into bankruptcy. Glasshouses Mill in its heyday employed 400 people under a benevolent management, but was not able to bear comparison with Saltaire; it was perhaps just not big enough to survive when the economic storms arrived.

George Metcalfe's great achievement was to persuade the railway barons to extend a spur up to Pateley Bridge, opened in 1862. Apart from other benefits this was in effect the start of the tourist industry in the Dale. However, there would be some harsh surprises. Economies of scale would favour competition from outside the Dale in such products as alcoholic beverages, for example.

The Industrial Revolution created a demand for a change of emphasis in two ways in education. First, competent adults were needed to manage and maintain the new machinery and technologies. There was no time to wait for a generation of youngsters to "come through", so adult education via the Mechanics' Institutes became established, in Scotland first by Dr. Birkbeck after 1820, and then strongly in Northern England bringing assured status for those able to cope with the subject-matter. Second, religious studies and classical syntax were seen to be irrelevant to such concepts as close engineering tolerances, and for understanding of safe handling of chemicals, including explosives. Technical education had arrived, with the creation of aspirations to careers leading to posts of chief engineer, chief chemist, and toolmaker, for those who had the necessary flair. Mechanics Institutes were set up in the Dale from 1839 onwards, but the emphasis, as recorded by Jennings, was on provision of more basic education to make up for earlier deficiencies. Although fees were very realistic it was necessary to rely mainly on voluntary lecturers.

By about 1878, as far as Pateley was concerned, conditions were really quite civilised. The effluent problem was being piped away, adult education was increasing the local store of saleable skills, the railway brought goods and services which helped to make life more congenial. Coal-gas lighting and heating transformed other areas. Leisure-activity as a concept made its appearance. An appropriate marker was the Cocoa House in Mill Road, later Millfield Road, which opened in 1880. A cast-list of those involved reads like a stage-army of the Good. There were many meetings of the steering group in the second half of 1879. The prime mover was the Honourable Henry E. Butler of Eagle Hall, who later inherited the title of Lord Mountgarret. He was supported by John Yorke of Bewerley Hall, and by three Reverends. William Harker of Harefield Hall and the Bradford Old Bank, Ltd., was there, as was Hanley-Hutchinson of Grassfields House, Viscountess Mountgarret of Nydd Hall, George Metcalfe of Castlestead and Doctor Edward Warburton.

The prospectus indicated the wish for a meeting-house without connection to religion or politics, to make available food and non-alcoholic beverages, with library and reading-room, a billiards room (snooker was not invented until 1889) and some rooms for overnight accommodation, with a resident manager. The venture opened as a limited company. Of the 1000 x £1 shares issued, 815 were taken up by about one hundred subscribers. Attempts to sell the balance of the shares failed, but the trawl for investors resulted in some families being represented more than once. Isaac Sinclair was a shareholder. The minutes reveal that the first application for the post of manager was from Thomas Blackah of Greenhow Hill, but he was not appointed, and soon after this rebuff Thomas went to live in Leeds. Dr. Warburton died in 1880; John Yorke in 1883. Another entry of interest is that John Bayne Newbould was contracted to do some of the fitting-out work in the building. The project sought voluntary liquidation in 1893, just before the Gouthwaite dam-builders hit town.

Rudyard Kipling was born in 1865, and somehow acquired enough knowledge of lead-mining on Greenhow to be able to write with such authority on the subject by the time he was 25 in 1890 when his short story was first published. He is known to have visited friends in Skipton deriving from the time his grandfather was a Methodist minister at Pateley Bridge. How marvellous to think he might well have listened to Thomas Blackah holding court in his little shop on Greenhow Hill near the Skipton-Pateley Road.

Thomas Blackah's writings under the pseudonym of Natty Nydds were reminiscent of Dickens's Sketches by Boz. In fact, making due allowance for setting and dialect, there are marked similarities between the Pickwick Club and the Ancient and Learned Society of Antiquarians. The former appeared in 1837 when Thomas was nine years old. Many of Blackah's poems reveal his kind awareness of the plight of the less fortunate of the Dale's residents. Notably, one such is the following, taken out of dialect.

Willie's Welcome Home

Now, Willie. Put your wallet down
And come and have your tea.
It's very rare you have the chance
To eat with t'kids and me.
We've waited for you to come home
For nearly half an hour;
The bairns were frightened you'd got lost
Coming home across the Moor.

I wish your work was nearer home
Or we could move your way.
Your lads oft wish that they could see
Their father every day.
Poor things, they never go to bed
But what they fret and cry.
I try to comfort them, and say
You'll be home bye and bye.

One night, this week, young Mat began
Saying he would roam;
He moaned and worried all about
His Dad not coming home.
I never got a wink of sleep.
I thought that he might die.
I cried myself, and would have given
The world if you'd come by.

I've washed and darned your stockings, love,
And patched your blue overalls,
And I've made a right good job
Of all your button-holes.
First thing this morning, when our Sal
Had washed the baby's suits,
She got the brush and blacking pot
And cleaned your Sunday boots.

I've six fresh-made pork pies for you;
That's one for every day.
You see, I don't forget you, love,
Although you're far away.
Home's so lonely through the week,
Until you're back again.
How badly off would women be
If they should lose their men.

Obviously, it is a kind poem, with a final punch-line charac-
teristic of folk-verse, but it may indicate why Thomas was content
to write for a local audience, behind a smokescreen of dialect.
Poetry and prose in the open literary market competed at that time
with the works of a range of giants, from Keats to Kipling, from
the Brownings to the Brontës.

Harald Bruff records that Blackah was extremely upset by an
incident which probably happened about 1865, when Thomas was
still recovering from his voyage to the New World. A discussion
arose at the *Miners Arms* as to whether or not there was a soldier
buried beneath a certain mound at the roadside on Coldstones,

which mound was always referred to as John Kay's Grave. There was a custom that one kicked the stones as one passed the mound, saying at the same time, "John Kay. Give me a knock." This was to let the soldier know that he was not forgotten. The oral tradition was that a company of soldiers from York had marched across Greenhow in 1812 on the way to Preston to assist the civil power in dealing with the Luddite risings. The day was very hot, and one soldier fell out and died on the roadside. Thomas Blackah actually helped his pals, including Moses Simpson and Will Longthorn, to open the mound to check the story, and about five feet down they found bones, a skull, and an old flintlock. Although they re-interred the remains and set up two stone markers, Blackah sought to make further amends by placing a suitable carving in the roof of Gillfield Level which passes directly below the place, and he was said to undergo a noticeable personality change as a result of his bad conscience about this matter. Buttons from the uniform were "trophies" for many years and one fell into the hands of Garnett-Jones some years after 1940. The story was told to Harald Bruff by Will Longthorn about 1918, when Will was about seventy-three years old. At the time Will also carried the oral tradition that a soldier of the Young Pretender's army had died in rather similar circumstances as the Scottish army of 1745 marched south, and was buried near Jacob's Well, close to the green road leading to West End. Nancy Millner informed Will, having herself had the details from her own great grandmother. These gleanings are derived from Harald Bruff's writings. Will was certainly Harald's chief informant, and the dates tie up because Will died in 1933, having celebrated in 1919 his golden wedding with his wife Hannah. As a young man he was involved in delivering stone to the site for the building of Greenhow Church which was consecrated in 1857. Will was born in 1839, ten years after Thomas Blackah, and they dug up John Kay about four years before Will's marriage in 1869.

Thomas Blackah lived out his last years in Leeds, and died there in 1895. Levi Gill spent his last years in Halifax, and was buried there in 1880, but one has the feeling that both Levi and Thomas probably thought of Nidderdale as home.

In his book, *T 'ill*, Harald Bruff said he had hopes of setting up a memorial to the way of life of the miners. He "gathered together bits of furniture such as they used, and odds and ends of tools and things useful and ornamental, with the intention of putting these into an old tumbledown miner's cottage bought for the purpose." Sadly, his hopes were not fulfilled.

CHAPTER 5

Diary of a Voyage in 1857 from Greenhow Hill, Pateley Bridge, to America

by Thomas Blackah and Members of his Family

IN WRITING AN account of a voyage to a foreign country, the narrator ought to have a good education, be well educated and have a good knowledge of the geographical position of the country which he has visited. But it is not the case with the writer of this small and short narrative, he only having had an imperfect education, being the son of a poor yet honest lead-miner.

★   ★   ★   ★

On the first of June 1857, I, along with eleven others, started from Greenhow Hill, a small village in the West Riding of Yorkshire, for Upper Canada in North America. The party consisted of my wife and two children, a brother-in-law and two children, a second brother-in-law and wife, and three single young men. We parted from relatives and friends about two o'clock in the morning, we walked to Skipton, a distance of twelve miles, accompanied by my father, two younger brothers and a few other friends. We arrived at Skipton and took the railway train about 8 o'clock in the morning for Liverpool, and bid adieu for a time to friends and relations 'mid tears and feelings known only to those who have been in the same position.

We arrived safely in Liverpool about three o'clock in the afternoon and took our luggage to No 5 Leeds Street, a boarding establishment kept by a gentleman by the name of Howard. We found it a very comfortable place, highly recommendable to all emigrants. We intended to take passage to New York in a steam vessel called the *City of Baltimore*. When we got to the booking office the berths were all taken up, so of course we had to take another vessel. The first that sailed was a Clipper vessel named *Ellen Austin*, belonging to the old Black Star Line. She was a large vessel commanded by Captain Garrick, bound for New York. We took a passage in the second cabin, but little did we know what we should have to endure on that vessel. We went on board on the 8th. of June in the morning. When the hurry and bustle attending placing the trunks and boxes in a proper position had subsided, the officer commenced serving out provisions, but what was our surprise to have 7 biscuits (1 lb weight), 1 lb flour, 1 lb oatmeal, 1 lb rice, 1 lb peas, 1 lb sugar, a small piece of tea, half gill of vinegar, 6 potatoes, 1 lb beef, 1 lb pork for a week's supply. The beef was either horse's or elephant's flesh. When it was well boiled 3 times it was still not possible to eat it. We cut it (with a deal of trouble) into small pieces so as it could be swallowed without much chewing. As for the pork, it looked as if it had been buried in the earth then taken out and washed (not clean) but about half clean. The rice and peas were moderately good, the flour was bad and dirty, the oatmeal very bitter. After provisions were served out we prepared to pass our first night on board a vessel. We had no lamp in our cabin as it was not allowed while the vessel was in dock. We slept very well the first night. When we awoke in the morning about five o'clock we had to go for our allowance of water; it was not so very good but we were forced to have it or nothing; there was some crushing and squeezing to get supplied one before the other. We got about three pints each for a day. In the forenoon a steam tug came and towed us into the river. We cast anchor but the wind was so strong they durst not venture into the ocean. In the afternoon a boat came with about 50 steerage passengers. When the hustle attending the arrival of the fresh passengers has subsided, a fresh one started up in the steerage. The officers caught a young man smoking below deck so they took him before the first mate – he ordered him to be taken on to the poop and tied by the hands to the mast.

We went to bed the second time and slept very well; we had a lamp in the cabin until about 10 o'clock and then the officer appointed to look after the passengers came down cursing and swearing that if we did not go to bed he would take us on deck and put us in irons.

We were forced to comply to any request they chose to make to us. Next morning at 5 o'clock they came cursing and swearing that if we did not get up they would pull us out of bed. We got up to a fresh bustle when they were serving out water. We expected to start into the main ocean on our voyage but the wind continued very boisterous so they durst not venture out. During the night a child was born on the vessel and one of the mates was put in irons for being drunk.

The next day a fresh company of passengers arrived and with them some orange women. They charged extra prices for their oranges and lemons and we found out for the first time that if we bought anything on board we should have to pay dearly for it. In the afternoon all passengers were called on deck and a search was made for anyone that was hid and wanted to go without paying. They only found one, a young man about 18 years of age; they took him before the Captain and kept him in the hold till the boat returned. The passengers were all driven on the poop and a man stood in the centre of the vessel with a list of all the passengers in his hand. He called out the names and another stout ruffian with a cane in his hand stood among the passengers calling out the names and kicking and striking them towards the forecastle using all kinds of taunts and abusive language to them, the very people who were paying their money that he was receiving to support himself. And all this done in the port of the first shipping town of civilised England. After all was done the boat returned and took this brute, supposedly a man, back with it together with the young man before mentioned, but before he went the mates bedaubed his hands and face over with tar and paint and they took him to Liverpool like that.

On the morning of the 12th. the steam tug arrived about 8 o'clock to tow the vessel into the ocean, at the sight of which almost every face beamed with joy; we were all tired of remaining in the river. About 600 human beings crowded within so small a compass, it was almost wonderful to think how we could live together 37 days. All was confusion and uproar while the seamen got the tug rope fastened to that little object that was to propel so large an amount of human beings, trunks, provision barrels, water casks (if they could call it water). It was that bad and obnoxious, although only a few days old. When they were serving it out at one end of the vessel you might smell it at the other.

But it was wonderful to behold the little tug carry the vesel with such ease although scarcely a twentieth of the size. It was a fine day and the scenery looked delightful as we came down the river Mersey. Behind was the thriving town of Liverpool, the mercantile metropolis of the known world. On our left was Birkenhead with its famous docks, with masts of vessels towering into the air for many a yard; further west was New Brighton with its fine park and beautiful buildings. Close to the water edge stood a noble lighthouse built on the solid rock and just beside it stood a stone Battery mounted with cannon that ranged the whole river. Before us lay St. George's Channel, the terror of all seamen in rough weather, and further west beyond the reach of his main vision lay the North Atlantic Ocean, where lay the bones of human beings without number.

The tug brought us as far as Holyhead on the Isle of Anglesey and from there it returned and left us to the mercy of wind and wave. We then bid farewell to old England expecting to see it no more for a time, if ever. We thought we had then got through the worst trouble attending emigration, but we soon found out we were only just going to meet it. As yet none of us was seasick but when the wind sprung up at night moderately brisk, then commenced the noise of people vomiting, some moaning, others praying, some cursing, some singing, laughing, talking, children screaming, the sailors singing their musical sea songs, and some of the sailors had good voices. If they had been properly trained they need not have been buffeted about on the ocean. Although they were negroes they were good natured and civil fellows.

When morning arrived the doctor came down cursing and swearing worse than a potter. If those who were seasick did not rise immediately he would drag them out of bed and what with vomiting and purging it would almost have suffocated a horse. They were laid in almost every position imaginable; the deck was almost tenantless and there was no crushing and thrusting to the cooking galley as there had been the previous days. Very few wanted any meat that day.

We passed between the Welsh and Irish coasts but we were that distance off both of them we could discover nothing with the naked eye. Towards night the wind got right ahead of us so they were obliged to tack the vessel for the first time. We went to bed at night mid oaths and curses as usual. We had got quite used to it now and expected nothing else, nothing particular having transpired during the latter part of the day. About midnight we encountered a heavy gale and the vessel began rocking and creaking first rate, boxes began rolling about, cans and bottles were rattling in all directions. Some passengers were thrown out of bed, men and women were shouting out that the vessel was going to sink. Women and children were crying for help on all sides. The Captain and Mates shouted out their orders, the sailors sung away at the ropes as if nothing were up more than common. We had a large crew on board. The Captain's name was Garrick, the first Mate's Kennedy, the second Mate's Wray, the third's Ledger, the fourth's Parker. There were three Boatswains, the first was Jones an Irish man who abused the sailors very ill, striking and kicking them without any provocation whatever; the second a yellow Boatswain, a fine handsome looking fellow who could speak German and French fluently; and the other was a black, middle aged man possessed of some property in the States. There were near 30 sailors, all negroes, and 20 cooks, persons working their passages over and they were very ill-abused, scarcely ever having a whole skin, especially their faces. I think if the Masters of the vessels only saw what the passengers and sailors had to endure (without they had hearts as hard as stone), they would have Captains and Mates with feelings of human beings instead of imps, for some of them would disgrace the brute creation, to be ranked among them. There are exceptions undoubtedly but they are very scarce.

The next morning was the time appointed for serving out our rations and this produced a fresh hurry and bustle on the vessel as many had finished their allowance two or three days since and were eager to be supplied as soon as possible. It caused a great deal of crushing that would not have occurred if they had had sufficient provisions allowed, for according to the Bill of Fare on the tickets there ought to have been plenty allowed to sustain nature. If anyone had money to get more he had to pay an extraordinary price for it.

A stone of flour cost 5 shillings and when they got it it was only a ship's stone. Currants and raisins were a shilling per lb. and they would not weigh more than nine or ten ounces; treacle about eighteen pence a pint (they did not weigh it); sea biscuits 6 for a shilling and they were so black and hard it was like eating tainted wood. Ale and porter was one shilling a bottle, port wine six, brandy five, gin and whisky four shillings per bottle.

There were only two cooking galleys for the passengers. The fires were kindled about 8 a.m. and put out at 4 in the afternoon, so there was not much time for cooking the little provisions we got. We were one day sat in our cabins very quietly talking about friends and home when we heard a crash in the air path into our cabin. It was the Captain's child, a fine little boy about 5 years old. He had been playing on the poop with a little wooden toy horse and the air path having been accidentally left open he fell through it – a distance of about 5 yards. The first Mate came running down the ladder at full speed. Happily the child had received no injury, only a little frightened. The Captain, in the heat of passion, swore that the first man who left it open again he would shoot him.

In a little time after this when we had got settled, the first Mate and Jones the Boatswain commenced beating a sailor for not scraping the masts right. They took both hands and feet to him and his face was so bruised they could hardly tell what it was like. It would have pitied the heart of a stone to have seen him if it was possible. After they had beaten him until they were tired, they sent him up again and kept him there till dark without anything to eat. The poor fellow took it all very patiently.

Towards night a large quantity of porpoises came about the vessel. The sailors pretend to know what part the wind will blow from by the direction the porpoises sail. They say they always keep their heads towards the wind. But we prove this to be a fallacy many a time during our passage there and back. Whenever we were becalmed, if we saw any porpoises the wind always happened to rise just after, but it would have risen if we had not seen the porpoises. There is one thing that is true, when the wind is going to rise the sailors know, but any of the passengers could know the same. In a calm the water is very smooth and looks light coloured, but when the wind begins to rise it begins by ruffling the water and as the breeze gets nearer they may see the effect of the wind on the water by the small waves coming nearer and nearer and by stirring the water it makes it look dark coloured. This explains the mystery of the weather wisdom which the sailors pretend to have.

One night a young child died. It was buried the next night. Its parents were Irish Catholics. A large company assembled round the berth of the bereaved ones, and spent the whole night in drinking and carousing one with another. They raised such an uproar singing, screaming, dancing and laughing, it was more like a madhouse than a place of mourning. We were informed that it was a regular thing with those people on such-like occasions. This was carried on down in the steerage; if it had been in the cabin they would have had them all in irons before morning.

On the fourth watch one day, Mr. Parker, the fourth Mate and Jones the Boatswain, were on duty. Jones commenced beating the sailors as usual when Parker begged him to desist and not abuse the poor men so. Then Jones commenced beating him most shamefully, Kennedy the first Mate encouraging him to do it. Jones cursed and swore he would pay him off for it after. It passed off for the present, only to be renewed in a tenfold more awful manner at night. About midnight there was such an uproar, oaths and curses accompanied by cries of murder. The first Mate and Jones made an attack on Parker in the dark, they nearly killed him outright. After some of the passengers had got to the scene of the action, the first Mate swore he would kill him outright if he spoke another word. In the morning when it got light, Mr. Parker appeared on deck with his face all cut and bruised most awfully. The Captain could not but know all the concern, for Parker was made Boatswain and Jones made fourth Mate in his place. What suffering has many a poor creature to endure on the ocean, if everything could be brought to light. When we had sailed as far as the banks of Newfoundland it became very foggy so they kept one sailor constantly on the forecastle blowing a large horn to give warning to any vessel which might be near, and another sailor at the bell, so that either the bell or horn was constantly sounding. But with all the precautions they can use, it sometimes happened that two vessels come into collision. It was very foggy the second day and blew a strong gale from the south west. The sea was high, and the vessel was sailing at the rate of ten knots an hour when a man on the look-out shouted, "A sail on the lee bow". Mates and men all rushed to the lee side of the vessel, and just when all became confusion the vessel clung to the weather side passing within fourteen yards one of the other. All the passengers that could get, rushed on deck to see what was up, but the vessel had disappeared in the fog. This narrow escape brought down on the man on the watch almost a small volume of oaths and curses from the Captain and first Mate. Instead of thanking the Almighty for such an intervention of mercy, they appeared to be trying which of them could excel the other in awful blasphemy, but such was the degraded state in which those men had fallen into, nothing whatever could make them consider anything for a moment but devilry and wickedness.

The weather continued foggy all the way over the Banks. When we got to the other side we were becalmed almost every day. Sometimed we just moved, at other times we had a dead calm. What agony of mind and body did we endure on that vessel, not knowing but we might be kept in it many a week, for the pox appeared to be doing its work with redoubled fury as the air began to be very hot during the day time, and at night it was so chilly and cold it was not possible to keep warm. Our cabins began to be noxious and we could get nothing to clean them with. There were thousands of flies of almost all descriptions, they could not be kept out of our meat. One day we were all called on deck and the officers pretended to clean below deck. They found some members' mugs occupied with excrement; they brought them out and cast them overboard. It was fine fun for the children, every fresh splash in the water brought forth fresh cheers from the younger fraternity of passengers who were very numerous, especially Irish.

We were becalmed one day; the sea looked white and smooth, there was not a wave to ruffle it. The sun was more than commonly hot, scores of little birds about the size and colour of martins gambolled around the vessel. It was really delightful, not a sound could be heard but the hum of human voices. The sailors were engaged tarring the ropes but there was no cursing and swearing by the mates as was the case when the wind was up and brisk. Far away in the distance the water appeared ruffled and coloured as it gradually came nearer and nearer till within a short distance of the vessel it proved to be but a shoal of mackerel. The place where they were appeared all life and motion, and presently two huge whales made their appearance spouting up water many a yard high and then disappearing for a short time. They rolled their monstrous bodies over so they looked like large boats, bottoms upwards. They came right among the shoal of mackerel and remained among them about half an hour devouring them by scores and hundreds at a mouthful. After they had disappeared in the distance came two black Sharks the very image of cunning and ferocity. They kept at a short distance from the vessel for two or three days successively. They did not appear to mind the small mackerel, for they appeared to be abundant in the waters near the fishing banks; every day we could see them surround us on every side.

It was very hot one day; the sailors were all engaged tarring the ropes. When one of the oldest of them had finished his bucket of tar he came to the first Mate for more. So the uncultivated ruffian began to make game of him, as he called it. I dispute that a fiend out of Hell could have behaved so to a human being. He made the poor fellow put his hands into the barrel of tar and stir it up with them. He then made him take them out, take his hat off and put it to his breast. The he had the poor fellow's tar-brush in the barrel stirring it up with it, and when he was stuffing his hat into his breast he rammed the tar brush right between his eyes. He then made him wipe the tar off his face with his tarry hands and he commanded him to his work following him on the deck, daubing his neck and face with the tar brush. The poor fellow was forced to take it all without saying a single word, if not he would have got well beaten and perhaps put in irons. One day Jones the Boatswain commenced abusing one of the sailors; the poor fellow begged of him to desist. The first mate came up at the same time and heard him, so they both commenced kicking and beating him as hard as they could. They struck him with short pieces of rope right over his face and head till he had to lie down for it, and then they took their feet to him while he was laid on deck insensible. When they were satisfied of abusing him, they left him for dead. The other sailors had him to carry to his berth; he was so abused he was forced to lie in bed till the first night watch was called on duty. When they were called out it would have pitied the heart of a stone to have seen their dejected looks. The mates were more than commonly severe. They cursed and swore they would kill them all before morning, and used all kinds of horrid language. When it got about dark they ordered the passengers below deck. We all thought there was going to be something up more than common for the first Mate walked about the deck with a large Newfoundland dog at his side, and the second Mate and Jones the Boatswain close behind him. After a while there was a rushing towards the Cooking Galley. Jones the Boatswain and the first Mate met the poor sailor who they had nearly killed earlier that day; they both commenced "full drive at him" with both hands and feet as usual. The poor fellow cried out Murder for all his might; the other sailors all made out of the way expecting it would be their turn the next for no one was safe on this awful ship. At the cry of Murder there was a rush of passengers on deck, the uproar it produced brought the Captain onto the Poop. He asked Mr. Kennedy what was "up". The passengers roared out there was cruel work going on, and Mr. Kennedy after studying for an excuse said: "Nothing, Sir! only a sailor fallen over a spar." This seemed to settle all, for the Captain walked his way back again. After he was gone into his cabin, the two Mates and Boatswain came among the passengers enquiring who it was that interfered with them, if they could only make it out, they would put them in irons and keep them there, but no one would tell. All seemed to be disgusted with them. The night passed away without anything more to do. The next morning the second Mate, Mr. Wray, came into our cabin and appeared to be very communicative to some young women. When they made mention of the other night's work he "blew it quite light" and said "Black men could not feel it hurt the same as white men, they were like dogs and horses". Here was a specimen of "good breeding". What will the owners of vessels have to answer for when all things are investigated before the Bar of God, for employing and setting on such like brutes over the poor sailors? How will they meet the poor despised, abused and slowly murdered creatures? What a sad catalogue of crime will there be published when "all things done in secret will be brought to light". But no human mind can conceive it.

One night, an Irishman accused a German of "doing his business" in a corner of his bunk, so the officers and first Mate marched down into the steerage to fetch the delinquent before the Captain. When he had tried the case over, he ordered him to go and gather it up in his hands, bring it on deck, and cast it overboard. Of course he was forced to obey, so he landed on deck with a large handful; there were roars of laughter set up at him, but it was dark, which greatly accelerated the punishment of the "dirty beast". He was a stout young man and one might have thought by his appearance he would never have been guilty of such a mean and dirty act, but how many are there among the proud young fops of our country who are guilty of acts almost as loathsome?

When we were about 200 miles from New York we had a dead calm for many a day. There we lay on the water in that dirty vessel for nearly a fortnight surrounded by the most noxious smells that can be imagined, the sun almost shining perpendicular upon us in the daytime and our cabins almost filled with flies. It was in the month of July and our water had got so bad we could scarcely abide the smell of it. They had it in casks under the forecastle and closets. We had to go every morning down into the low steerage for it. Sometimes we got over the shoe tops in excrement and urine when going to fetch it. How the poor creatures in the low steerage could live was almost a miracle; well might the hospitals be all filled with people with smallpox for there were about fifty with it when we cast anchor in the river near Staten Island. After we had lain in this position near a fortnight, and seen shoals of porpoises and mackerel, and a large number of whales, besides two sharks which were our companions every day, the wind stirred and we soon discovered a pilot boat snaking towards us. How every countenance beamed with joy thinking that they would soon re-land, and then farewell to all troubles attending seafaring, but we were doomed to nothing but disappointments as will be seen in the sequel.

When the pilot had been on board three days, we came within sight of a steam tug. It was soon alongside the ship and after a short parley between the captain of the steam tug and ours the 'tow cord' was adjusted to the little thing and away it started with its huge load towards the New World. Every eye was stretched to its full extent to see land. After a while, we espied land to our left; it was an island called "Staten Island". As we came nearer to it, it looked delightful, fine green fields with here and there a tree in the middle of them and the hedgerows bedecked with flowers of almost all colours glittering in the sunshine. The buildings were painted nearly all colours. The island was literally filled with halls and mansions belonging to the nobility of New York, for Staten Island is to New York the same as New Brighton is to Liverpool, a place of resort and leisure. We saw for the first time the splendid steamboats of the New World; they looked like floating mansions as they cut through the water at a swift rate. As we kept moving slowly and steadily up the river fresh sights came before us. With seeing nothing but water for about a month, our spirits were cheered with the sight of land, almost as much as the Children of Israel when they saw the Promised Land. We passed a large battery on our right, and about a mile further another on our left undergoing repairs and enlargement. When it is finished it will have upwards of 200 guns.

The Quarantine Doctor came on board the vessel, and when he saw the state we were in he ordered the vessel to be anchored in the Quarantine Ground. Thus, when we thought of ending our troubles, a fresh one started up again, for we did not know what they would make of us, nor when we should be allowed to go onto land. A boat came for the sick and they took them right to the Marine Hospital on Staten Island. It was Sunday morning when we cast anchor in the Quarantine Ground and we could hear the church bells ringing on all sides of us, but there we lay in that miserable place surrounded by ruffianly fellows, and hearing nothing but oaths and curses, while we could see other people strolling about the river side or skimming over the water in pleasure boats. A little boat came to us with fresh bread to sell, but we had to pay dearly for it and we wanted water very ill. A few of us joined and bargained for them to bring us a barrel of fresh water. They would not bring one for less than 7s. 6d. so of course we were obliged to either pay it or do without water. But before he left the vessel he told us he could not bring it till next morning. After he had gone away, we were soon through eating our fresh bread and although it was rather bitter it tasted very well to us who had lived on sea biscuits so long. But we were made to understand the position, viz., we were quarantined. No one but the quarantine officers were allowed to have intercourse with us. The place where we were anchored was marked out with buoys and officers were stationed to see that none of us got away till the Pox abated, and also no person came near the vessel with provisions but those set apart for it. In the afternoon a boat came to us with spirit to sell. The officers (or police) who are always on the lookout soon espied it beside our vessel. So off they set towards us with a boat and three men in it. When the two men in the boat that were with us espied the police boat coming, they were off as fast as they could row (for they were both row boats) and the other after them, and a fine race they had, the passengers shouting and laughing as hard as they could. But they overtook the trespassers before they got to land and took them prisoners, but it caused a piece of nice fun. After a while another smuggler came, and a fresh race occurred, which ended in the capture of the trespassers as before.

After this we had not the company of another boat that day, only the doctor's. He told us we should all have to be vaccinated for the smallpox the next morning. During the night a boat arrived from New York, and they smuggled a young girl out of the vessel unknown to anyone. Her brother, having heard of the vessel arriving and being quarantined, was determined to release his sister, which he accomplished, but being found out later, he got six months' imprisonment for it. She was brought back to this Quarantine Ground and had to remain till the rest of the passengers were released.

About ten o'clock the next morning the boat came with the barrel of fresh water and it tasted so well that we almost burst ourselves with it. We filled all the cans and bottles we had and we were really worried with others that had not subscribed to it wanting to taste it. When Moses smote the rock in the wilderness the people could not be more clamoursome. Some of them actually kneeled down to lick up off the deck what was spilled, such was the state which the poor creatures were in. After a while three doctors arrived and all were called on deck to be vaccinated, both men, women and children. It was like a sheepwashing; children were screaming, mothers trying to pacify them, men were sighing, fearing to go through the operation. They were crushing and squeezing one against another, nearly all wishing themselves at home again, and well they might seeing what they had undergone and not knowing when there would be an end to it. It was noised about we should have to remain in quarantine sixty days. When the doctors had left the vessel and we had just got down to our cabins, we got orders to lock our trunks and boxes and come up on deck. This, when we were just going to get something to eat, we were forced to leave it. They wanted to burn some tar in the cabins to quench the smells and to stop the infection. They kept us hungering on deck till nearly night, and when we were released the fires in the galleys were all out so we had to do as we could, without any cooked meat that day. We ate the fresh bread and drank cold water with it. This being Monday, the day for serving out provisions, they served them out at night for one day; we got one biscuit, one potato and a small quantity of rice for the day's supply.

They told us to have all the trunks on deck by six o'clock in the morning, for the steam tug would come at that time to fetch us to the Quarantine Ground. We went to bed fully considering it would be our last night on that loathsome vessel; we did not care much what kind of place they carried us to, so long as we got on to land.

But we were doomed to have one more disappointment before we got safe on to terra firma. Another vessel cast anchor alongside us, which had started out of Liverpool the same morning that we did; it was called the *Albert Galatin* with near seven hundred passengers on it. They had the smallpox on board, but it did not rage as it did on ours. They had towards 20 with it, we had 50. Early the next morning we were throng making ready for our departure. As soon as half past five o'clock, all the trunks and boxes were up on deck ready for the steam tug. Beds, and all kinds of pans, kettles, dishes, pints, bottles, and membermugs were thrown overboard by the score at once. The water was literally covered with them. The children and younger end were fairly delighted with it all. Many who had been clothed with rags and barefoot all the voyage appeared quite respectable this morning outside, but within would be almost empty. Underneath their clothes were scores of living creatures; they could be seen parading the men's coats and women's shawls by numbers at once. It would almost make one's flesh cringe on their bones to see them. They were quite ugly looking creatures, the large ones were very bulky about the middle or centre of their bodies but gradually tapered off towards the head and tail. Most of them had a dark spot right on the centre of the back, all the other parts of them were a light grey.

At about six o'clock water was served out to any one that chose to fetch it. A boy about fourteen years of age was going down through the hatchway to fetch some when he slipped and fell down through the lower hatchway into the low steerage. He fell with his head against a water barrel. They brought him on deck and laid him on a piece of canvas. The doctor examined him and said he was dangerously hurt, having broken his skull and caused concussion of the brain. His nose was broken, and he had a good many teeth knocked out and they took him away to the hospital.

About ten o'clock the steam tug arrived and commenced loading the luggage. It was four in the afternoon when they had filled it, and only about half the passengers with their luggage could get on it then. We expected it coming again for the rest, but we were informed it could not come till the next morning. Nothing now remained for us but to spend the night as well as we could. We had not a bite to eat. And the worst was, as soon as the trunks were got up in the morning, the sailors were ordered to pull all the berths down and make ready for cleaning the vessel before she would be allowed to enter into port. Here we were with two children, one four and the other two years of age, not a morsel of meat of any kind nor a bed to lie down on. We had kept a little quantity of the fresh water we got the other morning, but it was poor support for an empty stomach. We asked the first Mate for something to eat for the children but the wretch did nothing but laugh at us. When the children wanted to go to sleep, we fetched two or three boxes down and took some of the clothes out of them to make a bed of. We laid some long boards across the boxes so they did for beds for the children and sittings for us. We got the night passed as well as we could, and in the morning the steam tug arrived to fetch us on shore. About noon we were all safely got on to the tug boat, and we gave a hearty farewell to that miserable vessel.

When we got to the Quay or landing stage, the women and children were all taken forward and the men had to stay and get the luggage to the Custom House. While taking the boxes off the boat one of them happened to fall into the water and it floated nearly a hundred yards from shore. A young Cornish man stripped himself and swam after it and brought it back. When we had got them all into the Custom House we were taken into the ground appointed to us, where the rest had gone the day before. We were guarded by officers all the way to see that none made their escape, for we found out we were now considered no better than convicts. When we arrived at the gates they were locked till we were all ready to come through; the passengers who had come the day before were at the gates ready with water for us. They welcomed us with a loud cheer. When we had got through the gate in the Quarantine Ground we found it about an acre in extent, surrounded by a wall nine or ten feet high, and we were told that anyone that made their escape were to get six months' imprisonment. After we had got settled a little we were all ordered to one end of the place and had to pass before the doctor one at once to be examined. He told us there would be some meat for us in a short time. When it came it was tea and bread; we scarcely knew when we had got enough. It was forty eight hours since we had a taste of meat of any kind. The children, poor creatures, were fairly ravenous. They brought the bread in a cart in long square loaves about a foot long, six inches broad and four thick; these were cut into four pieces and thrown into hampers.

All the women and children sat by themselves on the green at one end of the ground and the men at the other end. They were all arranged in rows, then there were two or three hamperfuls of tin pints brought and distributed amongst them. Afterwards they came down between the lines with the bread, throwing it in regular rotation all along as they came through. Afterwards came the tea, in large kettles or cans, and some female servants to serve it out. Many a time has the place rung out with roars of laughter when there has been scrambling among them for the bread which came towards them. There were young foppish gentlemen and ragged dirty looking creatures all dining together off one table, viz. the green sward.

After we had partaken of the tea and bread, we prepared for passing the night. The women and children were taken from among the men and put into a long wood building one storey high about forty yards long and eight broad. There were two doorways into it, one at the south end and the other nearly in the centre. It was lighted by nine windows, eight in the front and one at the north or far end. There was a row of iron bedsteads placed up each side, with straw beds on them. They had grey horse sheets for blankets. Into this place the women and children were put to spend the night as well as they could. The men were put into a building three storeys high, which stood at right angles to the other. Into this place we were forced to lie down on the floor, there being no bedsteads for us. The first night we lay on loose straw laid on the floor the same way they bed horses, wrapped up in grey horse sheets. Many of the men laid in the open air on the bare ground, but before morning they were almost worried with mosquitoes, a kind of gnat, which is very troublesome all over the United States. It is about half an inch in length of body, long legs and a large head. It is in shape nearly like a Ginnyspinner, its bite resembles that of a Clegg. There was also to be seen at night the 'Firefly'. Numbers of these little creatures were dancing and looked like sparks of fire for an instant and then all appeared dark again. No sooner could you get your eyes to the place where they appeared, than all was dark and another appeared in another direction.

Then morning arrived and we arose and got ourselves well washed in pure water which refreshed us very much. Before we got our breakfasts we had to pass before the doctor and it was nearly ten o'clock before we got any. When it came, we were all arranged in rows as usual, and we were ready half an hour before we got it owing to the women and children being served the first. Many a thought passed through my mind as I surveyed that mixed multitude. If it had been possible, I would have given the world to have been set down with my wife and two children at the home we had left, but that happy time never arrived, as will be seen hereafter. If every one that intends to emigrate could only see the misery that they have to endure, I am fully persuaded there is not one in a hundred would ever start with a family.

During this day the passengers from the other vessel *Albert Galatin* came on shore to the same place where we were. This addition made our number amount to near 1300. We had to fast till they all got settled, and then they got served before us, so it got to be nearly night before we got anything to eat. We only got two meals that day. When we had got the supper over we were ordered to a fresh shed at the north side of the ground. We had nothing but bare ground to lie on. The other ship's passengers took possession of our places where we lay the other night. When it set in dark they commenced playing and dancing, just as if they were at a country fair. About midnight they commenced fighting and raised a regular row. The officers went in among them armed with revolvers and they took several of the ringleaders into custody. That night eleven young men made their escape out of quarantine; they all belonged to the *Albert Galatin*.

The next day the first Mate belonging to the *Albert Galatin* came to see the passengers belonging to that vessel. They showed their respect to him by carrying him shoulder high all around the ground, cheering and waving their hats in all directions. This proved how well he had behaved to them on their outward passage. They were allowed to dance, sing, play, or do almost anything to keep up their spirits while on the sea. Their water and provisions were good all the way, they were supplied regular and had as much as they could eat and drink allowed, so no wonder about them being so pleased with the first Mate when he came to see them. But we had a different scene presented to our view before night. Mr. Kennedy, the first Mate belonging to our vessel *Ellen Austin*, came through the ground to see Jones the Boatswain who was with smallpox. He got nearly through the ground before the passengers were aware who it was. When they made him out there was a regular rush towards him. The Germans drew out their large knives, some armed themselves with large sticks or anything they could find, and after him they went; no doubt but they were cursing and swearing vengeance on him if we could have understood them. The officers and the doctor had a deal to do to keep them from following him into the hospital, but when they could not get after him they prepared themselves for his return. But in that they were frustrated for the doctor got him conveyed through some gardens in another direction, and a lucky hit it was. If he had come the same way back as he went, he would have been lynched as sure as eggs are eggs. His behaviour towards the passengers (especially the Germans and Irish) was horrible; he was a real fiend in human shape. He had no more feeling for a human being than a stone. He had that wisdom about him to never try the experiment again. The first Mate belonging to the *Albert Galatin* came every day.

We thus passed on in misery and sorrow until the twenty second of July, when we got orders to make ready for our departure for New York. When the doctor made it known, there was such a shout of joy raised as I shall never forget; every one of our passengers, men, women and children, followed him to the gates, cheering him all along, as far as they were allowed to go. He was a model of good nature and kindheartedness; we never met with one like him wherever we went, for it seems a general trait in the characters of all the Yankees to be as big rogues and sharpers as ever they can.

After breakfast we started for the Custom House. The steam tug was ready for us; after we had got through the gates of the Quarantine Ground, we felt like convicts that had just got their liberty after a long term of miserable servitude, although we had not been kept in chains and forced to labour, yet we had been hungered to all intent and purposes. When we got all the luggage onto the tug boat and were nearly ready for starting to New York, the second Mate, Mr. Wray, and the yellow Boatswain came to the boat to take a last look at the passengers. Wray left the first amid hisses and groans from all parts of the boat, although he was not as bad as the first Mate, yet he had behaved very badly to the passengers all the voyage. When the yellow Boatswain left, he was cheered as far as he could be seen; all the passengers respected him. He was always civil and courteous and will be long remembered by all who knew him. As we left Staten Island we cast many a long look at it. There in the hospital lay a brother with the smallpox and in the village adjoining the Quarantine Hospital was his dutiful wife, surrounded by strangers, not a person whom she knew to speak to. But she would not leave her husband, although she had two brothers and a sister going up the country whom she might have accompanied.

As we came towards New York we came past a little island on which stood a large battery, mounted with large ordnance. We landed at a place called Castle Garden, a large circular building stood in the centre of the garden which had formerly been used for a theatre. It was a splendid building. There was a large number of emigrants in it, for they are allowed to stay here six days if they choose, and no lodgings to pay. They have to find their own meat, but they can go away any time they think proper. We had to get our names registered, where we came from, where we were going, what age and what profession or trade. There was some crushing and squeezing here again; all wanted to be forward to where they intended settling.

We had booked ourselves for Toronto at Liverpool, by the New York and Erie Railway, so we had tickets to present to Messrs. Holman & Wilkie, 27, Greenwich Street. It was close beside Castle Garden so we had not much trouble to find them. When we got into Greenwich Street, instead of finding a fine-looking, well-paved street, it was dirty and all full of jolt holes, but we did not stay long in New York. It was three o'clock when we got in, and we took the steam boat to Albany at five. The steam boat was a fine built, clean and well finished-off vessel. It looked delightful sailing up the River Hudson, it being a fine summer's night.

As we left New York the river banks were very rocky, sometimes the rock would rise perpendicular to a great height, and here and there a small hut built on the water's edge. We had a band of music on board, composed of Englishmen; they enlivened the scene very much. When we arrrived at Albany it was eleven o'clock at night, so we could not see what sort of place it was. When we came off the boat we were close beside the railway depot so we got our luggage weighed and got straight into the cars. (The railway carriages are always called cars by the Yankees.) We were all that night, and the next day till night came, before we got out of them. We passed a great many places but none of them appeared to be in any way attractive. One place called Susquanha looked a pretty little place. When we arrived at a town called Corning (a miserable looking place) we were informed that we should have to stay there all night, and we were not sorry for we had not laid in a bed for forty six days and the thought of a night's rest almost refreshed us. Our luggage had to be out of doors all night for there was not a building of any kind about the station to put them in. We went to a lodging house, a wood building; judge what were our thoughts when we got into the house. There were only a few chairs in the house, so we let the women and children occupy what sittings there were, and we were obliged to either stand or sit on the bare floor. After remaining about two hours in suspense, we got our suppers which consisted of potatoes, beef and tea, for which we paid one quarter

92

dollar, the price we paid for every meal we got in the United States. When we were ready for bed, they showed us to our bedrooms and what was our surprise when we got into the room we had to spend the night in, the rooms were all open to one another. There were door places between them but no doors in them. We laid on straw beds, the candlesticks were glass bottles. The candles were put into the bottle necks and the bottles were placed everywhere where there was room for them. However there was plenty of air circulating in the place; we could see the stars through the roof. It was a wooden building only newly built; it looked well at the outside, but within it was a mere pig cote.

We started the next morning on our journey and rode till night. When we arrived at a large town called Rochester, we were informed that the train would go no further that night, so we should have to stay all night. When we had got our luggage on to the platform we were told that it would be conveyed to another depot about a mile and a half off. We were soon accosted with runners belonging to different hotels and lodgings.

One of them, an Irishman, was very troublesome, and he would have no naysay but we should go with him; he told the women and children to get into his omnibus and he would take them free of charge. We told him to leave them at the depot till we got there with the luggage. After they had gone, an Englishman came to us and told us he had taken them to an Irish hotel, and that he kept the only English hotel there was in Rochester. We went with the luggage to the depot, and when we got there we found his words to be true, so we fetched them away and went to the English hotel. It was called "Williams Hotel" within a few yards of the station where the luggage was. We found it a very comfortable place; the owners were a young couple from London. They had a good many well furnished rooms and excellent feather beds to lie on. This was the first night we had spent comfortably since we left England. It was a large brick building in a fine street right in the centre of the town. We felt ourselves at home. The master and mistress were very communicative; we learned from them that we had come at the wrong time for things were very dull in the "Canadas". We passed a very comfortable night and next morning we started on the railway. We rode about seven miles and found ourselves on the margin of Lake Ontario. This is a large freshwater lake between Canada and the state of New York; it is about two hundred miles long and about fifty or more broad in some places. It has a communication on the north side with the River St. Lawrence and on the south west the Niagara joins it with Lake Erie.

We were soon on board a steam boat that was in connection with the New York and Erie Railway; it was built like the pleasure boats at New York, having three decks. They are very comfortable and swift sailing boats. They burn wood for to work the engine with, and as soon as they had got in the regular supply they started across the lake for Coburg in Upper Canada. We saw numbers of vessels crossing the lake in all directions. After we had been on board a few hours we were informed that we could have our dinners for one quarter dollar. We were quite ready for it, so we went down into the saloon and got one of the richest meals we had got since we crossed the Atlantic. It consisted of beef, potatoes, mutton, pies, puddings, fowls or almost anything you choose to have. The cooks were blacks but we did not mind about that, for we found out that they knew how to cook as well if not better than white people. The saloon was a fine large room, exceedingly well furnished; there were in it three large glittering chandeliers, two large superb mirrors, a large quantity of elegant chairs and numerous other costly articles. It was quite sufficient for any gentleman to dine in. When we wanted to drink we could go to the pump and pump as much as we wanted. It had a very good taste but was warm, it being a very hot day.

We arrived at Coburg about five o'clock and had to leave this boat as it came no further but returned to Rochester. A boat would come from Kingston past Coburg and we were told we should have to embark for Hamilton, but when it would arrive at Coburg they could not tell. We must hold ourselves in readiness for it. So, of course, we got our luggage piled up on the quay and went into the town. It was a pretty little place and we were told that everything was very dull. There was very little building going forward. As we had come from England to the lead mines near Toronto, we made enquiries after them but were told there was never such a thing heard of there. We went to a coffee house and got something to eat, and then went on the quay. It was a fine evening and when the people got to hear that there was a company of emigrants arrived, they came to see us by the scores. Everyone enquired where we came from. There were about twenty of us and we had all kinds of questions put to us. The natives were chiefly Irish and by far the greatest bulk of them wished themslves in old Ireland again.

★　　★　　★　　★

CHAPTER 6

An extract from "On Greenhow Hill" by Rudyard Kipling

first published in *Harper's Weekly*, August 1890

RUMBOLDS MOOR stands up over Skipton town, and Greenhow Hill stands up over Pately Brig. Moors and moors and moors, with never a tree for shelter, and gray houses with flag-stone rooves, and peewits crying, and a windhover (kestrel) going to and fro. And cold! A wind that cuts you like a knife. You could tell Greenhow Hill folk by the red-apple colour of their cheeks and nose tips, and their blue eyes, driven into pinpoints by the wind. Miners mostly, burrowing for lead in the hillsides, following the trail of the ore vein same as a field-rat. It was the roughest mining I ever seen. You'd come on a bit of creaking wood windlass like a well-head, and you was let down in the bight of a rope, fending yourself off the side with one hand, carrying a candle stuck in a lump of clay with the other, and clicking hold of a rope with the other hand. And then you came to a level, where you crept on your hands and knees through a mile of winding drift, and you come out into a cave-place as big as Leeds Townhall, with an engine pumping water from workings that went deeper still. It's a queer country, let alone mining, for the hill is full of those natural caves, and the rivers and the becks drops into what they call pot-holes, and come out again miles away.

I was a young chap then, and mostly went with horses, leading coal and lead ore; but at the time I'm telling on I was driving the waggon-team in the big sump. I did not belong to that countryside by rights. I went there because of a little difference at home, and at first I took up with a rough lot. One night we had been drinking, and I must have had more than I could stand, or happen the ale was none too good. Though in them days, By for God, I never seed bad ale. Nah! I never seed the ale I could not drink, the bacca I could not smoke, nor the lass I could not kiss. Well, we mun have a race home, the lot of us. I lost all the others, and when I was climbing over one of them walls built of loose stones, I comes down into the ditch, stones and all, and broke my arm. Not as I knawed much about it, for I fell on the back of my head, and was knocked stupid like. And when I come to mysen it were morning, and I were lying on the settle in Jesse Roantree's house-place, and Liza Roantree was setting sewing. I ached all over, and my mouth were like a lime-kiln. She gave me a drink out of a china mug with gold letters – "A Present from Leeds"– as I looked at many and many a time at after. "You are to lie still while Dr. Warbottom comes, because your arm is broken, and father has sent a lad to fetch him. He found you when he was going to work, and carried you here on his back." sez she. "Oa!" sez I; and I shet my eyes, for I felt ashamed of mysen. "Father has gone to his work these three hours, and he said he would tell them to get somebody to drive the tram." The clock ticked, and a bee comed into the house, and they rung in my head like mill-wheels. And she gave me another drink and settled the pillow. "Eh, but you are young to be getten drunk and such like, but you won't do it again, will you?" – "Noa," sez I, "I wouldn't if she'd not but stop they mill-wheels clattering."

And then Dr. Warbottom comes riding up, and Jesse Roantree along with him. He was a high-larned doctor, but he talked with poor folk same as theirsens. "What's ta bin agaate on naa?" he sings out. "Brekking tha thick head?" And he felt me all over. "That's none broken. Tha nobbut knocked a bit sillier than ordinary, and that's daaft eneaf." And so he went on, calling me all the names he could think on, but setting my arm, with Jesse's help, as careful as could be. "You mun let the big oaf bide here a bit, Jesse," he says, when he had strapped me up and given me a dose of physic; "and you and Liza will tend him, though he is scarcelins worth the trouble. And tha'll lose tha work," sez he, "and tha'll be upon the Sick

Club for a couple of months and more. Doesn't tha think tha's a fool?"

And that was how I came to know Liza Roantree. There are some tunes as she used to sing – aw, she were always singing – that fetches Greenhow Hill before my eyes as fair as yon brow across there. And she would learn me to sing bass, and I was to go to the chapel with them, where Jesse and she led the singing, the old man playing the fiddle. He was a strange chap, old Jesse, fair mad with music, and he made me promise to learn the big fiddle when my arm was better. It belonged to him, and it stood up in a big case alongside of the eight-day clock, but Willie Satterthwaite, as played it in the chapel, had getten deaf as a door-post, and it vexed Jesse, as he had to rap him over his head with the fiddlestick to make him give over sawing at the right time.

But there was a black drop in it all, and it was a man in a black coat that brought it. When the Primitive Methodist preacher came to Greenhow, he would always stop with Jesse Roantree, and he laid hold of me from the beginning. It seemed I was a soul to be saved, and he meant to do it. At the same time I jealoused that he was keen on saving Liza Roantree's soul as well, and I could have killed him many a time. And this went on till one day I broke out, and borrowed the brass for a drink from Liza. After fower days I come back, with my tail between my legs, just to see Liza again. But Jesse were at home and the preacher – the Reverend Amos Barraclough. Liza said naught, but a bit of red come into her face as were white of a regular thing. Says Jesse, trying his best to be civil, "Nay, lad, it's like this. You've getten to choose which way it's going to be. I'll have nobody across ma doorstep as goes a-drinking, and borrows my lass's money to spend in their drink. Hold tha tongue, Liza," sez he, when she wanted to put a word in that I was welcome to the brass, and she was none afraid that I would not pay it back. Then the Reverend cuts in, seeing as Jesse were losing his temper, and they fair beat me among them. But it were Liza, as looked and said naught, as did more than either of their tongues, and so I concluded to get converted.

Yon preacher Barraclough – a little white-faced chap with a voice as would wile a bird offan a bush, had a way of laying hold of folks as made them think they had never had a live man for a friend before. You never saw him, and – and – you never seed Liza Roantree – never seed Liza Roantree ... Happen it was as much Liza as the preacher and her father, but anyways they all meaned it, and I was fair shamed of mysen, and so I become what they called a changed character. And when I think on, it's hard to believe as yon chap going to prayer-meetings, chapel, and class-meetings were me. But I never had naught to say for mysen, though there was a good deal of shouting, and old Sammy Strother, as were almost clemmed to death and doubled up with the rheumatics, would sing out, "Joyful! Joyful!" and that it was better to go up to heaven in a coal-basket than down to hell in a coach and six. And he would put his poor old claw on my shoulder, saying, "Doesn't tha feel it, tha great lump? Doesn't tha feel it?" And sometimes I thought I did, and then again I thought I didn't, and how was that?

There was one thing the Methodists boggled at, and almost shut the gate in my face for, and that were my dog Blast, the only one saved out of a litter of pups as was blowed up when a keg of mining powder loosed off in the store-keeper's hut. They liked his name no better than his business, which were fighting every dog he comed across; a rare good dog, with spots of black and pink on his face, one ear gone, and lame on one side with being driven in a basket through an iron roof, a matter of half a mile.

They said I mun give him up because he were worldly and low; and would I let myself be shut out of heaven for the sake of a dog? "Nay," sez I, "if the door isn't wide enough for the pair of us, we'll stop outside, for we'll none be parted." And the preacher spoke up for Blast, as had a liking for him from the first – I reckon that was why I come to like the preacher – and wouldn't hear of changing his name to Bless, as some of them wanted. So the pair of us became regular chapel-members. But it is hard for a young chap of my build to cut traces from the world, the flesh, and the devil all of a heap. Yet I stuck to it for a long time, while the lads as used to stand about the town-end and lean over the bridge, spitting into the beck on a Sunday, would call after me, "Sitha, when's tha going to preach, because we are coming to hear tha. Where's tha white choaker." I had to double my fists hard in the bottom of my Sunday coat, and say to mysen, "If it were Monday and I was not a member of the

Primitive Methodists, I would leather all the lot of yond." That was the hardest of all, to know that I could fight and I must not fight.

So what with singing, practising, and class-meetings, and the big fiddle, as he made me take between my knees, I spent a good deal of time in Jesse Roantree's house-place. But often as I was there, the preacher fared to me to go oftener, and both the old man and the young woman were pleased to have him. He lived in Pately Brig, as were a goodish step off, but he come. He come all the same. I liked him as well or better as any man I had ever seen in one way, and yet I hated him with all my heart in the other, and we watched each other like cat and mouse, but civil as you please, for I was on my best behaviour, and he was that fair and open that I was bound to be fair with him. Rare good company he was, if I had not wanted to wring his cliver little neck half of the time. Often and often when he was going from Jesse's I would see him a bit on the road.

It is a way we have in Yorkshire of seeing friends off. Yon was a friend as I did not want to come back, and he did not want me to come back neither, and so we would walk together towards Pately, and then he would set me back again, and there we would be wal two o'clock in the morning setting each other to and fro like a blasted pair of pendulums twixt hill and valley, long after the light had gone out in Liza's window, as both on us had been looking at, pretending to watch the moon.

I was the first with Liza, and you would think that were enough. But the parson were a steady-gaited sort of chap, and Jesse were strong on his side, and all the women in the congregation dinned it to Liza that she were fair fond to take up with a wastrel ne'er-do-weel like me, as was scarcelins respectable and a fighting dog at his heels. It was all very well for her to be doing me good and saving my soul, but she must mind as she didn't do herself harm. They talk of rich folk being stuck up and genteel, but for cast-iron pride of respectability there's naught like poor chapel folk. It is as cold as the wind on Greenhow Hill – ay, and colder, for it will never change. And now I come to think on it, one of the strangest things I know is that they could not abide the thought of soldiering. There is a vast of fighting in the Bible, and there is a deal of Methodists in the army; but to hear chapel folk talk you would think that soldiering were next door, and the other side, to hanging. In their meetings all the talk is of fighting. When Sammy Strother were stuck for summat to say in his prayers, he would sing out, "The sword of the Lord and of Gideon." They were allus at it about putting on the whole armour of righteousness, and fighting the good fight of faith. And then, atop of it all, they held a prayer-meeting over a young chap as wanted to enlist, and nearly deafened him, till he picked up his hat and fair ran away. And they would tell tales in the Sunday-school of bad lads as had been thumped and brayed for bird-nesting on Sundays and playing truant on week-days, and how they took to wrestling, dog-fighting, rabbit-running, and drinking, till at last, as if it were an epitaph on a gravestone, they damned him across the moors with, "and then he went and listed for a soldier", and they would all fetch a deep breath, and throw up their eyes like a hen drinking.

I had no particular thought to be a soldier in them days, but this sort of talk put it in my head. They were so good, the chapel folk, that they tumbled over the other side. But I stuck to it for Liza's sake, specially as she was learning me to sing the bass part in a horatorio as Jesse were getting up. She sang like a throstle hersen, and we had practisings night after night for a matter of three months.

Most Greenhow Hill folks played some instrument or other, and they all sung so you might have heard them miles away, and they were so pleased with the noise they made they didn't fair to want anybody to listen. The preacher sung high seconds when he was not playing the flute, and they set me, as had not got far with the big fiddle, again Willie Satterthwaite, to jog his elbow when he had to get started playing. Old Jesse was happy if ever a man was, for he was the conductor and the first fiddle and the leading singer, beating time with his fiddle-stick, till at times he would rap with it on the table, and cry out, "Now, you mun all stop; it's my turn." And he would face round to his front, fair sweating with pride, to sing the tenor solos. But he were grandest in the choruses, wagging his head, flinging his arms round like a windmill, and singing hisself black in the face. A rare singer were Jesse.

You see, I was not of much account with them all excepting to Liza Roantree, and I had a deal of time setting quiet at meetings and horotorio practices to hearken their talk, and if it were strange to me at the beginning, it got stranger still at after, when I was shut on it, and could study what it meaned.

Just after the horotorios came off, Liza, as had allus been weakly like, was took very bad. I walked Dr. Warbottom's horse up and down a deal of times while he were inside, where they would not let me go, though I fair ached to see her. Then they said if I was quiet I might go in, and the Reverend Amos Barraclough used to read to her lying propped up among the pillows. Then she began to mend a bit, and they let me carry her on to the settle, and when it got warm again she went about same as before. The preacher and me and Blast was a deal together in them days, and in one way we was rare good comrades. But I could have stretched him time and again with a good will. I mind one day he said he would like to go down into the bowels of the earth, and see how the Lord had builded the framework of the everlasting hills. He was one of them chaps as had a gift of saying things. They rolled off the tip of his clever tongue. I lent him a suit of miner's kit as almost buried the little man, and his white face down in the coat-collar and hat-flap loked like the face of a boggart, a hobgoblin, and he cowered down in the bottom of the waggon. I was driving a tram as led up a bit of an incline up to the cave where the engine was pumping, and where the ore was brought up and put into the waggons as went down by themselves, me putting the brake on and the horses a-trotting after. Long as it was daylight we were good friends, but when we got fair into the dark, and could nobbut see the day shining at the hole like a lamp at a street-end, I feeled downright wicked. My religion dropped all away from me when I looked back at him as were always coming between me and Liza. The talk was that they were to be wed when she got better, and I could not get her to say yes or nay to it. He began to sing a hymn in his thin voice, and I came out with a chorus that was all cussing and swearing at my horses, and I began to know how I hated him. He was such a little chap, too. I could drop him with one hand down Garstang's Copper-hole – a place where the beck slithered over the edge of a rock, and fell with a bit of a whisper into a pit as no rope in Greenhow could plump.

Ay, he should see the bowels of the earth and never naught else. I could take him a mile or two along the drift, and leave him with his candle doused to cry hallelujah, with none to hear him and say amen. I was to lead him down the ladder-way to the drift where Jesse Roantree was working, and why should he not slip on the ladder, with my feet on his fingers till they loosed grip, and I put him down with my heel? If I went first down the ladder I could click hold on him and chuck him over my head, so as he should go squashing down the shaft, breaking his bones at every timbering as Bill Appleton did when he was fresh, and hadn't a bone left when he wrought to the bottom. Niver a blasted leg to walk from Pately. Niver an arm to put round Liza Roantree's waist. Niver no more – niver no more.

But it is none so easy to kill a man like yon. When I had given up my horses to the lad as took my place and I was showing the preacher the workings, shouting into his ear across the clang of the pumping engines, I saw he were afraid of naught; and when the lamplight showed his black eyes, I could feel as he was mastering me again. I were no better nor Blast chained up short and growling in the depths of him while a strange dog went safe past.

"Thou art a coward and a fool," I said to mysen; and I wrestled in my mind against him till, when we come to Garstang's Copper-hole, I laid hold of the preacher and lifted him up over my head and held him into the darkest on it. "Now, lad," I says, "it's to be one or the other on us – thee or me – for Liza Roantree. Why, is tha not afraid for thysen?" I says, for he were still in my arms as a sack. "Nay; I'm but afraid for thee, my poor lad, as knows naught," says he. I set him down on the edge, and the beck run stiller, and there was no more buzzing in my head like when the bee comes through the window of Jesse's house. "What dost tha mean?" says I.

"I have often thought as thou ought to know," says he, "but it was hard to tell thee. Liza Roantree is for neither on us, nor for nobody on this earth. Dr. Warbottom says – and he knows her, and her mother before her – that she is in a decline, and she cannot live six months longer. He has known it for many a day. Steady, John! Steady!" says he. And that weak little man pulled me further back and set me against him, and talked it all over quiet and still, me turning a bunch of candles in my hand, and counting them over and over again as I listened. A deal on it were the regular preaching talk, but there was a vast lot as made me begin to think as he were more of a man than I had ever given him credit for, till I were cut as deep for him as I were for mysen.

Six candles we had, and we crawled and climbed all that day while they lasted, and I said to mysen, "Liza Roantree hasn't six months to live." And when we came into the daylight again we were like dead men to look at, and Blast came behind us without so much as wagging his tail. When I saw Liza again she looked at me a minute and says, "Who has told tha? For I see tha knows." And she tried to smile as she kissed me, and I fair broke down.

You see, I was a young chap in them days, and had seen naught of life, let alone death, as is always awaiting. She told me that Dr. Warbottom said that Greenhow air was too keen, and so they were going to Bradford, to Jesse's brother David, who worked in a mill, and that I must hold up like a man and a Christian, and she would pray for me. Well, they went away, and the preacher that same back end of the year was appointed to another circuit as they call it, and I was left alone on Greenhow Hill. I tried, and I tried hard, to stick to the chapel, but it was not the same thing at after. I hadn't Liza's voice to follow in the singing, nor her eyes a-shining acrost their heads. And in the class-meetings, they said I mun have some experiences to tell, and I hadn't a word to say for mysen.

Blast and me moped a good deal, and happen we didn't behave ourselves over well, for they dropped us and wondered however they had come to take us up. I cannot tell how we got through the time, while in the winter I gave up my job and went to Bradford. Old Jesse were at the door of the house, in a long street of little houses. He had been sending the children away as were clattering their clogs in the causeway, as she were asleep.

"Is it thee?" he says; "but you're not to see her. I will not have her wakened for a nowt like thee. She's going fast, and she mun go in peace. Thou'll never be good for naught i' the world, and as long as thou lives thou'll never play the big fiddle. Get away, lad, get way!" So he shut the door softly in my face.

Nobody never made Jesse my master, but it seemed to me he was about right, and I went away into the town and knocked up against a recruiting sergeant. The old tales of the chapel folk came buzzing into my head. I was to get away, and this was the regular road for the likes of me. I enlisted there and then, took the Widow's shilling, and had a bunch of ribbons pinned in my hat.

But next day I found my way to David Roantree's door, and Jesse came to open it. Says he, "Thou's come back again with the devil's colours flying – thy true colours, as I allus telled thee." But I begged and prayed of him to let me see her nobbut to say good-bye, till a woman calls down the stairway, "She says John has to come up." The old man shifts aside in a flash, and lays his hand on my arm, quite gentle like. "But thou'll be quiet, John, for she's rare and weak. Thou allus were a good lad."

Her eyes were all alive with light, and her hair was thick on the pillow round her, but her cheeks were thin – thin to afrighten a man that's strong. "Nay, father, you may not say the devil's colours. Them ribbons is pretty." And she held out her hands for the hat, and she put all straight as a woman will with ribbons. "Nay, but what they are pretty. Eh, but I would have liked to see thee in thy red coat, John, for thou was allus my own lad – my very own lad, and none else."

She lifted up her arms, and they come round my neck in a gentle grip, and they slacked away, and she seemed fainting. "Now you must go away, lad," says Jesse, and I picked up my hat and I came downstairs.

The recruiting sergeant were waiting for me at the corner public-house. "You've seen your sweetheart?" says he. "Yes, I've seen her," says I. "Well, we'll have a quart now, and you'll do your best to forget her," says he, being one of them smart, bustling chaps. "Ay, sergeant," says I. "Forget her."

And I've been forgetting her ever since.

CHAPTER 7

An Epilogue for the Millennium
(With acknowledgements to Percy Bysshe Shelley)

Yorke's Folly a.k.a. Two Stoops
by Ken Wilford

A man told me as I hiked north from Leeds:
Two huge, man-made but broken, columns stand
On the rim of Nidd Dale. No hint of creeds,
They view all points; the site well-chosen for command.
Like Troy, what seem to be foundations may
Have yet an older base. The Legions tramped nearby;
Of that we can be sure. Now overlain, not far away
The die-straight cobbled roads their deeds do signify.
A telling legend can be read on one half-buried stone:
"We rule this land to vision's end, from this our mighty throne.
Kneel to our works, ye tyrants, and despair."
But nought much else remains. Round the decay
Of that abandoned pile, rock outcrops bare
And bleak and lonely moors stretch far away.

Index of Persons Mentioned

Adair, Septimus 15
Appleby, Charles 60, 64
    Jon 30
Atkinson, John 49
    Stephen 6, 49

Bartlett, Archd'n 27
Bayne, Ann 39, 46, 47
    Joseph 33, 45, 47
    William 45
    William C. 47
Baynes, John 47
Bendigo, 53, 54
Benson, Bridget 24
    Christopher 24
    Edward W. 24
Bentley, David 33
    Dorothy 39
Birkbeck, 67
Blackah, Thomas 18, 54, 65, 66, 69
Blakeborough, Richard 26, 65
Blakeney, Percy 58
Bolton, Emma 40
Boston, Emma 40
Bowes, Jimmy 56
    John 56
Bradford, John 65
Bradley, George 25, 27
Brayshaw, 16
Brown, Tom 25
Bruff, Harald 23, 51, 53, 55, 56, 58
Buck, Wilfred 49
Burgous, David 49
Busfield, James 12
Butler, Henry E. 68

Calverley, Edward 40
    James 40
    John 39
Calvin, John 18, 22
Carlyle, Thomas 17, 67
Cayley, Sir George 30
Chambers, John 49
Chaucer, Geoffrey 28
Christie, Julie 29
Clark, Joseph 3
Coates, Bob 54
Coleridge, Samuel 17
Cooper, Ann Ashley 65
Courtenay, Tom 29
Cowling, George 49

Dacre, Jackey 7
Dearden, John 38
Dickens, Charles 23, 69
Dickenson, Jacky 13
    Mrs. 13
Didd, Tailor 8
Dodd, Sam 57
Dunn, Mrs. 13
Dougill, Susey 42
Dunbar, Revd. Peter L. 49

Eyles, John 41

Fearnly, 16
Ford, John 29
Foxton, Carl 22, 30, 49
    William Edgar 30
Furniss, Thomas 24

107

Gill, Alfred Ward 19, 20, 43
  Alice 20
  Ann 1, 20, 24
  Ann (Nanny or Nancy) 33, 44,
    46, 48, etc.
  Ann Elizabeth 40
  Clara 20
  Dorothy 33
  Edward 1, 10, 20, etc.
  Edward Levi Joseph 21, 57
  Edwin 13, 36, 37
  Elizabeth (Betty) 19, 20, 33, 36
  Hannah 33, 36, 49
  Henry 20
  Herbert 41
  Jane 20 33, 42
  John 40
  John Edwin 20
  Joseph 24, 40, 41
  Levi 1, etc.
  Malley 33, 38, 39
  Mary 34, 38
  Mary Ellen 20
  Matthew 20, 31, 33, etc.
  Nelson 13, 36, 40
  Robinson 31, 36, 37, 43, etc.
  Sarah 41, 44
  Tom 35, 44, 52
  William 4, 10, 14, 20, etc.
Gillance, John 49
Grainge, William 2, 9, 18
Grange, Christopher 4
  Kit 4
  Thomas 2
Groves, Ann 39
  Jane 41

Hardcastle, Jacob 49
Hardy, Thomas 49
Harker, John 2, 7, 9
  Robert 2, 7
  William 68
Harrison, John 8
Hawksworth, John 40
Hazlitt, 17
Hebden, Judith 63
Hewitt, Joseph 16
Hick, Elizabeth 40
Hill, Sir Rowland 32

Holdsworth, Joseph 49
Holgate, Revd. Ralph 14, 22, 23
Holmes, Thomas 49
Homer 28
Horner, Joseph 49
Hunter, George 49
Hutchinson, Hanly 68

Ingham, Ann Elizabeth 40
  William Gill 19, 43
  Thomas 40
Ingleby, Joseph 13, 24
Irving, Washington 50

Jackson, William 3, 26
Jennings, Bernard 22, 24, 52
Johnson, Joe 29
Jones, Edward T. 23
  Garnett 23, 24, 71
  John Paul 58
  Peggy 23, 27

Kay, John 71
Kendal, William 38
Kilburn, John 41, 54
King, William IV 64
Kipling, Rudyard 31, 69
Kirkbride, Betty 55

Lascelles, Edwin 28
Leach, 16
Leeming, Joseph 40
Lofthouse, John 49
Longstaff, William 49
Longthorn, Hannah 71
  Will 63, 71
Longthorne, William 63
Lush, Ernest 24

Mawson, Grace 40
Marsden, Robert 49
Metcalfe, Elizabeth 67
  George 23, 34, 66, 67
Millner, Nancy 71
Milward, James 49
Moulson 15
Mountgarret, Viscountess 68

Nelson, Elizabeth 33
Nettleton, Thomas 49

Newbould, John Bayne 47, 68
  William 26
Nickleby, Nicholas 25

Orczy, Baroness 58
O'Shaughnessy, Mary 21
Outhwaite, Matthew 29

Paley, James 9
Pedley, Dyson 49
  Luke 49
Perry, Patricia 18, 21, 49
Pratt, George 55
  Jamie 55

Queen Anne 5, 20, 30
  Victoria 26

Ransom, Joseph 49
Rawnsley, Sam 15
Ripley, Jane 39
  John 33, 49
  Nelson 39
Robinson, 33

Scaife, John 2, 26
Simpson, Moses 71
Sinclair, Elisha 61, 62, 63
  Henry 64
  Jack 60, 61, 62, 63
  John 64
  Mary 63
Slavin, Ellen Cecilia 21
Slinger, George 49
Snow, Richard 25
  William 13
Snowden, Isaac 15
  Joseph 15
  Thomas 15
Squeers, Wackford 23
Stead, 15
Stephenson, George 25
Stones, George 3, 44
  Matthew 45, 46, 49
  Thomas 3, 8, 49
Strodder, Doctor 11

Sugden, Doctor 12
  William 15
Sunter, Pedley 53, 55
Sutcliffe, James 16
Swires, Dayne 64
Swires, John 1
  Muriel 22
  Wiliam ("Old") 1, 22, 23

Thompson, William 53
Thorp, Ann 33, 39, 44
  George 42
  Grandmother 2
  Jane 39, 42
  John 42
  Joseph 42
  Uncle 12
  William 39, 42
Tilburn, Edward 41
  John 40, 41
Treadwell, Elizabeth 19, 40
Trees, William 49

Verity, Gregory 42
  John 42
  William 42

Waddington, Jonathan 16
Walton, Thomas 15
Warburton, Dr. Edward 12, 31,
  66, 68
  Dr. Joseph 11, 12
Ward, Anthony 33, 38, 39
  Edward (Ned) 38
  Henry (Harry) 38
  William (Bill) 38
Waugh, James 15
  John 15
Wayne, John 29
Wesley, John 29
Wilson, Mathew 59, 63
  William 3, 26
Wood, Joseph 15

Yorke, John 22, 23, 47, 60
  Squire 2, 34, 64

Index of Places Mentioned

Abbey Lodge 49
Albany 85
Aldershot 54
Angkor Wat 51
Arthington 53

Beeston 28
Bendigo, Aus. 53, 54
Bewerley 2, etc.
  Hall 2, etc.
Blaydon 59
Blazefield 62, 66
Birmingham 26
Bolling 15
Borobudur 51
Bowling 7,15
Bradford 7, 9, 14, 24, 27, 41, 67
Bramhope 53
Bridgehousegate 1, etc.
Brompton Hall 30
Brooklyn, U.S.A. 31, 36
Bruce House 44, 46
Burton on Trent 40

Canada 59, 73
Canterbury 24
Castlestead 34, etc.
Church, Lancs. 42
Cocoa House 68
Coldstones 70
Cornwall 52, 54
Craven Moor 51

Dallowgill 4, 17, 29, 66
Darlington 30
Dry Gill 52, 55

Eagle Hall 68
Edinburgh 17, 58
Eshton 63
Eton 24

Fountains Abbey 48

Gillfield 71
Glasshouses 67
Gouthwaite 69
Granada 50
Grantley 43
Grassfields House 68
Grassington 22
Great Marlow 54
Greenhow 2, etc.
Guyscliffe 41

Halifax 21, 40
Hardcastle 55
Harefield Hall 68
Harewood 28
Harrogate 25, 29, 33
Hartlepools 58
Headingley 45
High Wild Carr 62, 64
Huntley, Aus. 41

Inns and Pubs:
  Barley Mow 7
  Bowling Green 13, 28
  Crown 13
  Dry Gill Public 52
  Grouse 52, 54
  Junction 16
  Miners 53, 54

Inns and Pubs:– *cont.*
Perseverance 15
Queen's Head 54
Shoulder of Mutton 2, 13
Sun 8
Ireland 32

Keld Houses 55, 65
Kell House 62, 65
Kirby Malzeard 62, 66
Kirkstall 6
Knaresborough 29, 44

Laverton 62
Leathley 40
Leeds 4, 5, 27, 29
  Briggate 5, 30
  Corn Exchange 30
  Park Row 30
Liverpool 73
London 17, 21, 34, 66

Manningham 8, 15, 46
Masham 26
Mechanics Inst. 29, 68
Middlesmoor 42, 45, 55

Newfoundland 79
New York, Yorks. 9, 18, 39
New York, U.S.A. 17, 36, 46, 49,
  57, 83
Niagara 94
Nidderdale 2, etc.
Norwood 27
Numurkah, Aus. 41
Nydd Hall 68

Otley 32, 40

Pateley Bridge 1, etc.
Peterborough 39
Pyramids 51

Richmond, Sur. 29
Richmond, Yorks. 23

Ripley 47
Ripon 28, 46
Russia 55

Sandhurst, Aus. 41, 54
Sawley 43
Scarborough 29, 58
Sheffield 38
Shepherds Bush 29
Shepperton, Aus. 41
Shipley 8, 9
Ships:
  Albert Galatin 90
  City of Baltimore 74
  Ellen Austin 74
Skipton 26, 32, 73
Snowden 31, 38
Staten Island 84
Stockton 30
Summerbridge 64

Tanfield 26
Tasmania 61, 65
Thruscross 31
Thwaite House 45, 47
Timble 31, 46
Toronto 92

Undercliffe 16

Victoria, Aus. 41

Wakefield 28, 40
Wales 52, 54
Washburn, River 27
Washington, D.C. 58
Waterloo 50
Wath 35
Weedon, Northants. 19
West End 13, 36
Wilsill 23, 25, 42

Yeadon 44
York 15
Yucatan 51

111